THE
INTEGRATIVE
LEADER

How Leaders Use Both Sides Of Their Brain To Build Resilient Companies

SONIA JEANTET

INDIE BOOKS
INTERNATIONAL®

The Integrative Leadership Model™ is a pending trademark of Sonia Jeantet.
The Whole Brain Thinking Model® is a registered trademark of Hermann Global.

ISBN-13: 978-1-952233-37-1
Library of Congress Control Number: 2020924247

Designed by Joni McPherson, mcphersongraphics.com

INDIE BOOKS INTERNATIONAL, INC®
2424 VISTA WAY, SUITE 316, OCEANSIDE, CA 92054
www.indiebooksintl.com

THE INTEGRATIVE LEADER MODEL

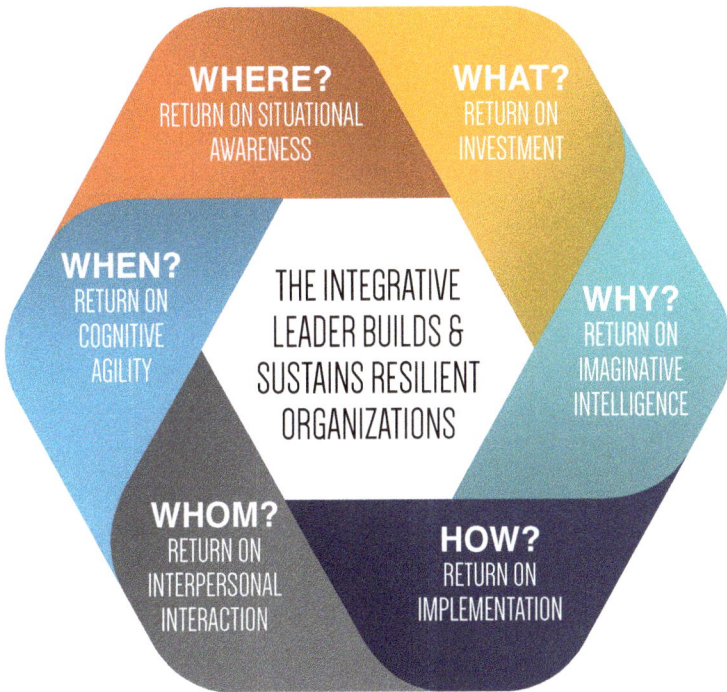

WHERE?
RETURN ON SITUATIONAL AWARENESS

WHAT?
RETURN ON INVESTMENT

WHEN?
RETURN ON COGNITIVE AGILITY

THE INTEGRATIVE LEADER BUILDS & SUSTAINS RESILIENT ORGANIZATIONS

WHY?
RETURN ON IMAGINATIVE INTELLIGENCE

WHOM?
RETURN ON INTERPERSONAL INTERACTION

HOW?
RETURN ON IMPLEMENTATION

CONTENTS

Preface vii

Part I: Why Integrative Leadership Matters 1

1   Why You Need To Use Both Sides Of Your Brain 3

2   How Smart Executives Become Integrative Leaders 15

Part II: How To Become An Integrative Leader 29

3   Optimize Your Return On Situational Awareness 31

4   Optimize Your Return On Investment 45

5   Optimize Your Return On Imaginative Intelligence 53

6   Optimize Your Return On Implementation 65

7   Optimize Your Return On Interpersonal Interaction 77

8   Optimize Your Return On Cognitive Agility . . . 89

Part III: Creating A Culture Of Integrative Leadership 101

9   How To Sustain Integrative Leadership 103

10 Into The Future Of Integrative Leadership . . . 111

Appendix 119

    Acknowledgments 119

    About the Author 123

    References Cited 125

    Index 127

PREFACE

Writing an insightful book that provides actionable intelligence to leaders everywhere has been a goal of mine for the past five years. The dilemma was finding the right topic and the time to dedicate to this important project. The inspiration for the content and coordination of my schedule came together in March 2020. The speed and depth of the changes everyone would experience due to the coronavirus pandemic created new neural pathways for all. Our expectations and plans for what we would get done this year professionally and personally changed practically overnight.

My time shifted from in-person client meetings to creating a tool for leaders everywhere. I suddenly had a dedicated period of time to apply what I have experienced in helping leaders become whole-brain thinkers. I am pleased to share *The Integrative Leader Model* that builds resilient organizations.

I have enjoyed dedicating a large portion of my days to capturing what helped my clients grow in their roles and achieve successful outcomes. Outcomes that reconfigured strategy, structure, processes, people, and technology quickly turned toward value-creating and value-protecting opportunities. This project fulfills more of my purpose to be an effective leadership performance partner. May you discover golden nuggets you can apply to your business, however different your day-to-day business may be from what you knew prior to March 2020.

Sonia Jeantet

July 2020

PART I

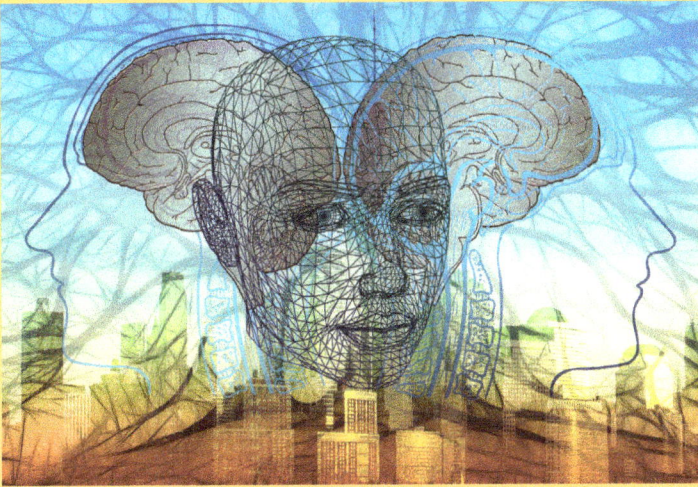

Why Integrative Leadership Matters

CHAPTER I

Why You Need To Use Both Sides Of Your Brain

"When faced with a storm, a tree that doesn't bend becomes wood."

—African proverb

We are living in transformative times for the entire world. There are overt and covert changes taking place to government structures, financial paradigms, social norms, industry composition, and geopolitical relationships. This is the perfect storm for breakdowns of long-established systems.

No one alive or in leadership has simultaneously experienced what has occurred in the first half of 2020. Events like a global pandemic, worldwide economic shutdown, demonstrations and riots lasting months across most of the cities in America and the world, and new protocols for resuming business are creating a new playbook for leading through a crisis.

Psychologists would inform us that any one of these circumstances would challenge our ability to cope because we are in deep survival mode. At the base of our head is a special location, the amygdala, from which chemical reactions emanate to deal with these circumstances. When we have an amygdala hijack, we revert to examining our world and actions, and the instinctual question of "How can I be safe?" dominates our decision-making and behavior.

Fight, flight, and freeze strategies are at the top of the list in the midst of uncertainty and form the first phase of our response. The quicker we move through this phase, the greater our chances for assessing potential options to create a highly functioning future. The number and depth of the neural connections in the frontal portion of the brain, where you do your best thinking, evaluating, and understanding, will determine your ability to thrive in the unfolding new world.

This book shows how leaders, when faced with complex business challenges, applied cognitive diversity that delivered optimal financial and organization results. Six of the chapters will highlight a factual story of a leader applying a left-, right-, or whole-brain solution to resolve their circumstances. Chapters three through nine will also refer to a thought leadership source that validates the results achieved by the leader.

This information will be relevant to two groups of readers: the owners and leadership of an organization, and the emerging leaders who want to avail themselves of all possible tools that will help them thrive regardless of the circumstances they face.

A surprising statistic from a study conducted by Accenture Strategy: 89 percent of C-Suite executives have degrees in left-brain directed fields such as engineering, finance, and accounting.

Importantly, there is a difference between left-brain thinking and right-brain thinking. In 1990, Hermann Global, an Inc. 500 firm, pioneered *The Whole Brain Thinking Model.*[1] The model has four quadrants to define thinking preferences, two for each side of the brain. According to this model, the left brain is analytical, logical, and focused on facts and form, while the right brain is the creative, innovative, emotional, visual-spatial half focused on futures and feelings. The relative level of activity in each quadrant is believed to determine an individual's cognitive style and personality.

Individual and team assessments reveal which quadrants an individual may favor. The firm's data indicates that leaders who have dominance in all four quadrants are least represented in the population. Yet, CEOs and presidents of organizations and divisions are more successful when they maintain a balance in their leadership priorities that take into consideration issues and opportunities in all four thinking styles.

In general, an executive's career experience tends to align with their dominant thinking preferences since

---

[1] Herrmann Global LLC, "Cognitive Diversity for Better Management," Herrmann, accessed May 2, 2020, http://www.thinkherrmann.com/.

they will play to, and be rewarded for, their strengths. This pattern is often correlated to the organization's industry. Industries where engineering and financial acumen are critical value left-brain preferences. Industries where innovation, interpersonal savvy, and curiosity are important complement right-brain thinking. There are connections between the upper mode of left and right, which emphasizes strategic thinking and innovation management. Clinicians and process implementers tend to have brain connections between the lower mode of both right and left brain. However, the knowledge and instincts that favor one side or mode over another do not have the same value today, because of the complexity in the workplace and the pace needed to affect change. An ambidextrous brain provides a significant advantage for leadership success.

I have been an executive coach for the past twenty years, consulting with such varied Fortune 500 organizations as Raytheon, Disney, and Warner Bros. I am engaged to work with high-potential executives. They are the individuals who have consistently proven themselves over the course of their career; they solve difficult problems and are instrumental in developing and launching new ideas, products, systems, and businesses. Their career path is in an upward trajectory. They are moving into larger leadership roles: running a new line of business, redefining how a product or service is provided, entering new markets, identifying and delivering against new return on investment models, and always growing the scope of the teams they lead.

Early in my coaching career, it became clear that a high-potential executive who began to practice and take on whole-brain thinking habits had a greater chance to be successful regardless of what their next role would be. That executive was being an integrative leader, leveraging the full potential of their thinking abilities. An integrative leader is in the optimal performance zone. Neuroscientists define this as a state of neural harmony where the disparate areas of the brain are in sync, working together. It is also defined as a state of maximum "cognitive efficiency" or being "in the flow," which lets you use whatever talent you have at peak levels. In this book, these concepts are illustrated with stories of high-potential executives with whom I have had the pleasure and honor to work.

To succeed in the twenty-first century, you and the executives on your team will have to operate as whole-brain thinkers. AI and robotics are tools that elevate the efficiency of what traditionally have been left-brain competencies, and in some cases, are replacing jobs that build that knowledge and experience. In addition, for right-brain competencies, there have been many initiatives for growing emotional intelligence to manage a diverse workforce generationally and across other distinctions. When I took the first emotional intelligence assessment, distinguishing among different visual cues for others' feelings was part of the test. It can be argued that the facial recognition feature in surveillance cameras and our phones is capturing that information to better understand and market to us. This is one example of how technology leverages a strong right-brain skill set. The advantage of being a fully functional human being is achieving and maintaining the whole-brain optimal performance zone.

Human beings are frequency generators and resonate with what is in our field. Our thinking is influenced by our environment. The more we interact and connect with machines, the more we are comfortable with structured thinking, which is a left-brain strength. The more we spend time interacting with others in conversations that explore imagination and build interpersonal connections, the more we are resonating with strategizing and personalized thinking, our right-brain strength. In the midst of complex situations that require breakthrough solutions, integration and balanced thinking across both brain hemispheres provide access to the field where the whole universe of options exists.

The change in neural pathways allows integrative leaders to embrace new behavior habits, which strengthens their ability to lead. The process for launching new neural pathways begins with the questions we ask ourselves. In his book, *Quiet Leadership,* David Rock shares, "The questions you ask of your brain significantly affect the quality of the connections it makes, and profoundly alter the patterns and timings of the connections the brain generates in each fraction of a second."[2]

---

[2] David Rock, *Quiet Leadership: Help People Think Better -- Don't Tell Them What to Do: Six Steps to Transforming Performance at Work* (HarperCollins Publishers, 2006).

It is what happens when we have an "aha" experience. The insights gained allow these leaders to recognize the situations they are facing and deftly shift to the optimum return for the organization, be it return on ideas, investments, interpersonal interactions, process, situational awareness, or cognitive agility. Some examples of the leadership skills modeled include the ability to synthesize diverse thinking and viewpoints; being vigilant to the external environment; making tough decisions effectively; and the ability to influence, coach, and empower others.

Understanding Return For Integrative Leadership And Research Validates

The twenty-first-century business environment is a brave new world. We will need a larger percentage of leaders who are practiced at cognitive diversity or whole-brain thinking. In *The Integrative Leadership Model*, they are integrative leadership practitioners.

Research conducted from February through April 2019 by Accenture Strategy[3] with 200 C-Suite executives, 5,700 consumers, and 5,700 employees in France, Germany, Italy, China, the UK, and the US defined the circumstances leaders will face. They will be challenged to solve complex business problems in new ways, with different constituents, at a new pace and scale, and with bigger consequences than ever before for getting it wrong.

---

[3] Peter Lacy, Katherine LaVelle, Alberto Zamora, "Striking Balance with Whole Brain Leadership – The New Rules of Engagement," Accenture Strategy research study, 2019.

Here is the view from the C-Suite:

- 85 percent say disruptive impact of new technologies has increased

- 74 percent say disruptive impact of constantly shifting customer demands has increased

- 72 percent say disruptive impact of new market entrants has increased

- 62 percent say investors are among their most disruptive stakeholders

- 49 percent say employees are among their most disruptive stakeholders

A banking board member in the UK shared: "Aside from the generally accepted skill sets that we feel are required for the kind of senior positions that we have, the next thing that is high on the list is cognitive diversity. All the evidence says if you can get a better level of cognitive diversity, you get a better outcome. You get better profitability. You get a better perspective on each problem that you are trying to solve."

From the *New Rules of Engagement for the C-Suite* 2019 research study, here are the whole-brain skills and behaviors C-Suite leaders demonstrate:

Figure 1

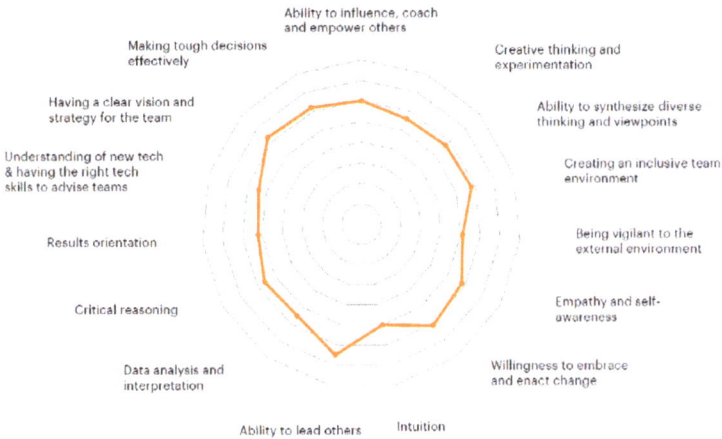

Ability to influence, coach and empower others
Making tough decisions effectively
Creative thinking and experimentation
Having a clear vision and strategy for the team
Ability to synthesize diverse thinking and viewpoints
Understanding of new tech & having the right tech skills to advise teams
Creating an inclusive team environment
Results orientation
Being vigilant to the external environment
Critical reasoning
Empathy and self-awareness
Data analysis and interpretation
Willingness to embrace and enact change
Ability to lead others
Intuition

The study revealed that only 8 percent of the C-Suite leaders use a whole-brain approach today.

The financial results of those who practice cognitive diversity report stronger average growth and profitability; +22 percent average three-year revenue growth and +34 percent average three-year profit (EBITDA) growth. As a result of the study, 82 percent intend to use a whole-brain approach in the next three years.

The choice for the boards and organizations that plan to thrive in these times is to address the skill gaps. *The Integrative Leader Model* I am sharing with you in this book can be used to re-skill C-Suite members and to build bench strength with talent recruited from the outside.

There is a silver lining for integrative leaders. This style of leadership attracts natural change agents who seek to be empowered. They are naturally predisposed to ponder and respond to disruption. This creates opportunities for leading in new dimensions and guiding them on building a vibrant, coherent, and resilient state for the organization. The organization's brand will have a new currency and relevancy.

At the end of chapter one and chapters three through nine, you will find tips for applying the information to grow integrative leadership skills. *The Integrative Leader Model* is a framework designed to enhance a leader's ability to build and sustain a resilient team, business, and organization. The recommendations provide a range of options that may require partnering with organization development or a skilled cognitive diversity consultant to implement. Applying the recommendations in the Becoming An Integrative Leader boxes will reveal whether that step in the model is a well-developed competency in your organization or a blind spot. For example, to use return on imaginative intelligence: the leader may not explore why the company is in the business often enough to recognize a breakthrough opportunity or replace the ineffective practices and habits that have built up over time.

I look forward to partnering with the organizations eager to embrace *The Integrative Leadership Model.*

BECOMING AN INTEGRATIVE LEADER

Administer a "thinking preferences" assessment to the leaders in areas where your business will be experiencing the greatest challenge, change, or complexity.

Partner with HR and/or a cognitive diversity consultant to create a library of critical skills for effective change and/ or managing complexity leadership.

Categorize the library into cognitive preferences (align with left/right brain) using the *Integrative Leadership Model*.

Build a cognitive diversity proficiency level grid for the critical leadership skills.

Build career paths that move emerging leaders through the proficiency grid.

Create a skill gap development plan with an experienced executive coach to raise the cognitive diversity performance for the leaders.

CHAPTER 2

How Smart Executives Become Integrative Leaders

A t a recent lecture at the campus of the University of California-Irvine, the career guidance speaker explained that your connection to work is either as a job, career, or calling.

Jobs are a transaction of your time for money and carry little additional investment by the employee or employer. They are subject to volatility as the market for a position changes in value. Technology is continually replacing jobs with robots and artificial intelligence.

A Career often involves training and learning to improve your skills such that you succeed and advance to the next level. Agile thinking and the results you deliver determine your path.

A Calling is an optimal alignment between your skills and talent to the position you hold in an organization.

You enjoy the process of achieving mastery and providing value. Growing in scope builds new neural pathways that expand your opportunities.

Challenges in the marketplace and the transformation affecting all aspects of the business and social environment require additional tools to thrive in your career or calling. Resilient organizations will navigate through uncertainty and change because of the abilities of their integrative leaders. Integrative leaders engage in cognitive diversity to deliver outstanding outcomes. They have built a plethora of mental models from both sides of the brain and synchronize them as needed to achieve successful results.

The next section will share a detailed look at how to become an integrative leader.

Before I give you a guided tour, you should meet your tour guide.

Sonia's Journey To Coaching Integrative Executives

My father shared that when I was three, he remembers me constantly asking, "*Que es esto*?" This is "What is it?" in Spanish, which is the native language of Bogota, Colombia, where I was born and raised.

The logical and analytical upper left part of my brain was seeking to identify the world around me. In a leader's scope of responsibilities, focus in this area is about the bottom line.

Later on, when I was about six years old, the word I used most often was "Why?"—which at times was a particular strain on my mother.

The integrating and synthesizing upper right side of my brain was trying to understand the big picture of my world.

Seeking to make sense of our world starts early. We activate the circuits in our brains to be successful in creating and achieving results we consider important. The journey an integrative leader takes is about deliberately activating the whole-brain patterns to become adept at solving ever more complex problems and thriving in any unforeseen situation.

"There are more possible ways to connect the brain's neurons than there are atoms in the universe."
—**John Ratey, 2001**

Taking American Express To Latin America

In 1979, American Express hired me into a nine-month preparation program to open credit card centers in Latin America.

There were fifteen other newly-minted International MBA graduates who, like me, spent time in every department, not only learning the business but engaging as free consultants to the leaders in those departments on what they could do to improve some aspect of their responsibility. Coming up with new solutions and cleaning up a hot mess always starts with questions. What? Why? Where? Who? How? And especially, When? Timing is critical to stop losses or launch an initiative that provides a strategic advantage. The actions taken may well impact the bottom line in the current quarter or business year.

Every department was a piece of the puzzle to forge a successful and coherent organization that delivered a solid return to the company. The insights I provided to each department manager were shared with my boss to determine if I was qualified to move to the next step. Upon completion of the program, there was good news and bad news. I was one of the few keepers. But the company chose to indefinitely delay opening up those centers.

I am forever grateful to American Express for launching my business career with professional experience to ponder and promote new ways to create positive returns for various departments. Every time I started in a new area and understood the in-place systems, I was making meaningful connections within and between systems. Their intention was that as the center manager overseas, I had well-grounded tools to build profitable results.

What I Learned At Hewlett-Packard

On my first day at Hewlett-Packard in 1982, the hiring manager gave me a leather-bound organizer. "I'm giving you peace of mind. You now have a place to organize your appointments, notes, and ideas."

I unzipped the organizer, and on the inside cover was a page entitled, "The HP Way."

The hiring manager smiled and said, "Here are the guidelines from Bill and Dave on how to be a successful employee and ambassador for the company."

Soon I learned that the HP Way was alive and practiced by all the people I collaborated with during my eight years with the organization. Although none of us met Bill and Dave during our time with the company, their imprint lived on decades after they defined it. We all adopted the practices and behaviors of a high-performance organization. My experience in that culture has made it easy to discern when those practices and behaviors are present in a company, division, team, and leader. When leaders use both sides of their brain, the basis for co-creating this high-performance culture is seeded.

The concept of creating and sustaining a high-performance culture became popular in the late 1990s. HP provided a good example, but companies pursuing it found replicating those results elusive because it is not a technique. What it *is* is described below.

In 2007, Michael Malone published *Bill & Dave – How Hewlett and Packard Built the World's Greatest Company* to inspire the next generation of entrepreneurs to design their organizations with their model in mind. Here is an excerpt:

Bill and Dave's management model is an ethos of restraint, responsibility, and, most of all, trust.... It sounds easy, but the HP Way is nearly impossible to execute because it demands forbearance by the very people most likely to aggrandize power and almost infinite trust from the people least likely to give it. When it works, as it did at Hewlett-Packard for decades, the HP Way creates a decentralized, cohesive, and intensely competent organization of stunning resilience—and a genius for innovating itself out of hard times. In the age of global organizations, independent work teams, and lightning decision cycles, the HP Way is better suited for modern organizations than any other. The HP Way was devised from a basic understanding of human beings—of duty, family, responsibility, inventiveness, and the desire to succeed and make a contribution.[4]

Malone provides context for those who lived the HP Way and captures the return it yielded. Building a successful career in a high-performance culture fueled my desire to share with leaders tools to grow their abilities, and to enhance the return on their career journey. At HP, cognitive diversity was encouraged and occurred when we collaborated to get the work done. We became more effective by understanding and valuing different thinking processes and ideas.

---

[4] Michael S. Malone, *Bill & Dave: How Hewlett and Packard Built the World's Greatest Company* (Pengion Group, 2007).

The Integrative Leader Model is my experience-wrapped roadmap for the journey of your top talent. Moving through the model assists in creating new neural pathways and experiences across the company. The sustainable imprint for those who participate will be about how the elements create a resonance that expands the field of opportunities.

Your business lives in an interdependent world that creates the most benefit when leaders are aware and accountable for how elements bond and blend together. Coherence within the organization sets the tone for a more congruent connection to partners and clients. This becomes part of your brand and opens doors and builds alliances.

Sharing knowledge and providing a forum for senior leaders to engage with other like-minded individuals was a perk provided by HP to our clients and qualified prospects.

I will never forget when a senior leader at Rockwell International accepted my invitation to a session in Palo Alto with a well-known thought leader. On the plane ride up, I asked, "Janie, why did you clear your calendar to attend the session?"

"I have heard from industry colleagues that attending these sessions has shown them how to do a better job," she replied. "If I'm able to ask myself a different question the next time I'm faced with an unexpected challenge or opportunity, it will be worth it."

She was looking for a return on ideas.

The Crossroad To Coaching

While working at Digital Equipment Corporation (DEC) in the mid-1990s, it was clear to me that this was a company in decline. I knew I did not want to jump to another company in the industry if I might have another possible path to optimize sixteen-plus years of successful experience and business development skills in technology. Early in my career, my father's counsel was, "You know it's time to leave a job or industry when the best of you does not want to show up for work every day." I called a former mentor to share my predicament.

He asked, "What else do you want to do?"

"I don't know," I whispered into the phone.

"You might want to ask a few people who know you well professionally and personally," he shared in an upbeat tone.

A lightbulb went off in my head. Of course. Create a survey and have people share what they knew and experienced from me. I selected twelve people: four industry colleagues, four former clients, and four relatives and friends. It took me two weeks to compile the responses and put them into a spreadsheet that would reveal any common themes. Here is what I learned:

- My teams are talented, strong, productive, and get along well

- I develop others well

- I seem happiest when people exceed their own limitations

The longer I looked at the list, the more I realized it suggested a career as a therapist or a trainer.

I shook my head in disbelief. I did not want to start my career all over again in such a new direction.

I needed something to take my mind off this dilemma. It was the first Thursday of the month when the art galleries in Laguna have their open houses. My favorite gallery was showing some new works from one of my favorite Venezuelan artists. None of my friends were available to accompany me, but a glass of white wine and viewing good art was all I needed.

I arrived early, meaning it was quiet, and I was not going to have to make small talk with strangers when I was in this pensive mood.

The artist Maria Beltran's works were beautiful. They were oil paintings of scenes in the Caribbean. The colors were vibrant and inviting. Maybe I needed a vacation there.

"Hi, do you own any of her works?" asked the professionally dressed woman standing next to me.

"Yes, do you?"

"No, but I am interested in this painting. You seem to appreciate it as much as I do. Are you going to buy it?"

"No, it was inspiring me to go on vacation there."

"Really? What do you do?"

"I'm in transition."

"You don't have a job?"

I laughed. "I do have a job, but it's not the one I want."

On a hunch, I decided to share my survey project and what the themes were from my raters.

A twinkle appeared in her eyes, and she said, "Oh, you should become an executive coach."

"An executive what?" I had never heard of that career.

"Executive coach. It's what people like me do when we want to work with high-functioning individuals."

"What is your profession?" I asked timidly.

"I'm a therapist. I own a trauma-counseling practice and work with business leaders when there is a traumatic event at their company. I would do more executive coaching but find that they perceive I don't understand their world because I have not been an executive at a company. Do you have a master's degree?"

"Yes, but it's in business, not psychology."

"But that's perfect. And there is one continuing education college I know here in California that provides executive coaching training. I'll be happy to arrange an introduction for you with the president."

On my drive home, I could not help wondering at this coincidence. The rest, as they say, is history. The following week, I spoke with Jeff Auerbach, the president of the College for Executive Coaching, and learned about the process. It took me a year and a half to earn my certificate.

Early in the journey, I asked Jeff what he considered was the yearly earning potential for a good coach. When he shared it was $40,000, I gasped. "Jeff, that is not enough for me. Plus, it does not make sense. If we are helping executives remove blind spots and become more effective, we are worth a lot more than that."

"What were you thinking?" asked Jeff.

"At least $100,000 a year."

"That will depend on your clients and experience. I'm sure seasoned coaches might be making closer to that figure, but it might take you five or more years."

Okay, I love a challenge. In my previous career, my success depended on being discerning and on how well I qualified prospective clients. I would fall back on that experience to build my practice.

> At the end of the second year, as I was reviewing the profit-and-loss statement for my business, I pushed the print button from QuickBooks, and in the gross profit box on my statement, $100,000 stood out.

"Yes!" I sang out.

In the past twelve years, I have guided high-performing executives on the journey to becoming integrated thought leaders, with results that exceeded their expectations, and on occasion, even my own. Now I would like to share the journey of six special integrative leaders I have had the good fortune to coach.

Coaching Process And Context

Organizations have hired executive coaches for the past three decades. In the beginning, coaching was more of an intervention to "fix" the leader's actions. The leader or executive lacked "fill in the blank" to be successful in their role, or worse, might be derailing. Coaching was the last step before the organization chose to part ways or limit the course of that leader's career.

Around 2004, organizations realized that investing in their leaders was the best purpose for engaging a coach, and the model shifted to working with executives who create bench strength and will be the future leaders of the organization. In an effort to gain support from the leaders to be coached, most companies adopted a "chemistry meeting" step at the beginning. Now, the leader is in charge of selecting the coach who they perceive will be their best partner for the journey.

The coaching process involves four steps:

Assessment. Online reports of style preferences and feedback from selected raters are used to create a 360-view (managers, subordinates, and colleagues) into the executive's strengths and weaknesses.

Development plan. Data from the assessment step is used to create an action plan for addressing the areas for improvement. This plan is shared with HR and the executive's sponsor—typically their manager. This provides support and engagement from HR and the sponsor.

Coaching to the plan. Meetings with the executive are held to share tools and engage in conversations around executing the development plan. The opportunity to share changes and challenges leads to many "just in time" coaching moments. Sharing a different point of view with the leader contributes to building new neural pathways.

Review the progress. Sharing the plan's accomplishments and progress with HR and the executive sponsor is done at the end of six or nine months with HR and the executive sponsor. Next steps are identified to help the leader sustain and build on what they learned and the new tools in their leadership arsenal.

Leadership Performance Partner

I am the founder of Cima Executive Development, a coaching and consulting firm in Southern California. I have been an International Master Personal and Executive Coach for twenty years, primarily with Fortune 500 companies. I work with senior executives to discover, align, and support the key management practices that grow and sustain profitable results. I am bilingual in Spanish and English, with strong experience and understanding of cultural differences. My clients include Cedars-Sinai, City National Bank (an RBC Company), Disney, Warner Bros., Raytheon, and Toyota.

Integrated Leader Competencies.

The next six chapters illustrate the journey integrative leaders navigate as they solve critical issues for the organization and grow cognitive diversity such that they amplify the return for the organization. You will uncover returns that you may not track at this time in your company, but will likely have a great impact on the results you achieve.

PART II

How To Become An Integrative Leader

CHAPTER 3

Optimize Your Return On Situational Awareness

Here is a surprising development:

> *In the recent past, the magnetic North Pole has moved thirty-four miles a year toward Russia. Just a half-century ago, the magnetic North Pole was wandering only about seven miles each year.*

n his February 5, 2019 article "Earth's Magnetic North Pole Has Officially Moved," Trevor Nace, PhD, geologist and *Forbes* senior science contributor, reveals the critical importance of location.[5]

Following is a summary of the article. Earth's magnetic North Pole has drifted so fast that authorities have had

---

[5] Trevor Nace, "Earth's Magnetic North Pole Has Officially Moved (Toward Russia)," *Forbes.com* (Forbes, February 5, 2019),

to officially redefine its location. Keeping this model current is critical in ensuring the accuracy of work in government and commercial organizations around the world. Specifically, NASA, the Federal Aviation Administration FAA, and the US Forest Service use the magnetic poles in their daily operations, from mapping to air traffic control. On a more individual level, smartphones use the magnetic north for GPS location and compass apps.

For geologists and scientists, maintaining keen situational awareness of true north is essential to all of us. Small errors on their part can translate into major problems and dysfunction for untold millions of organizations, systems, and citizens alike.

Understanding Return On Situational Awareness

To be able to choose the right future focus, you, too, need situational awareness. Situational awareness is defined as the perception of environmental elements and events with respect to time or space, the comprehension of their meaning, and the projection of their future status and impact. This requires the engagement and coordination of all parts of the thinking brain.

The magnetic North Pole for your industry is influenced by many factors. The industry and organization situational awareness step will inform you and your team of whether there are changes to your industry's compass that will affect your organization's current status and future plans for success.

Return on situational awareness requires strategic management. A common practice in high-performing cultures is "postmortem" meetings to understand what worked and why. The review of the recent financial results that got you to where you are now is evidence of current execution against the plan.

Completing the following steps will help you and your team understand the environment in which your company operates.

Conduct an external and internal audit. This includes:

- Define the current state of the business, i.e., start-up, reinvention, growth. A SWOT (Strengths, Weaknesses, Opportunities, and Threats) analysis lays the foundation for this step. An eighteen-month to two-year financial trend analysis reveals progress or opportunity gaps that will affect the business as conditions change for the customer or the organization. A big-picture review of the financial trends reveals the relationship between resources and return by the client. There may be out-of-balance conditions that need attention in a future model. These would include factors like reducing complexity, critical profit centers, ROI on investments, etc.

- Assess the current state of the industry, i.e., transition, inflection point, etc. Business development research on the industry mapped against the existing pipeline is a critical step for future-focused brainstorming.

- Sharpen the focus by making minor or major changes to the vision and mission.

- Identify the relevant top three priority issues you are facing now.

Research Validates

In January 2016, *McKinsey Quarterly* "Leadership in Context"[6] reviewed the survey results of 375 people from 165 organizations across multiple industries and geographies to gauge organizational health. Organizations were described as ailing, able, or elite. Competency and resilience are at the core of a healthy organization. These practices are necessary to respond to an unexpected shift in the marketplace.

Return on situational awareness is the cornerstone to create and maintain organizational coherence in the midst of change. Coherence aligns the relationship between functions and teams such that their plans and actions build on each other to produce a unified whole. Integrative leaders understand that the intelligence derived from identifying what has changed in the industry is critical to optimize results. The return on situational awareness will affect the direction, organization capabilities, accountability, and motivation.

---

[6] Michael Bazigo, Chris Gagnon, and Bill Schaninger, "Leadership in Context," *McKinsley Quarterly*, January 2016.

Exhibit 1

When a rigorous self-diagnosis isn't possible, these rules of thumb are helpful in assessing the health of organizations.

	Ailing	Able	Elite
Direction	Strategy fails to resolve tough issues	Compelling strategy reinforced by systems and processes	Sense of purpose and engagement about the vision
Leadership	Very detailed instruction and monitoring (high content)	Sensitivity to needs of subordinates (high support)	Stretch goals to inspire working at full potential (high challenge)
Culture and climate	No coherent sense of shared values	Baseline of trust within and across organizational units	Strong, adaptable organization-wide performance culture
Accountability	Excessive complexity and ambiguous roles	Clear roles and responsibilities; performance and consequences linked	"Ownership" mind-set encouraged at all levels
Coordination and control	Conflicting and unclear control systems and processes	Goals, targets, and metrics aligned and managed through effective processes	Value from collaboration captured and measured across organizational boundaries
Capabilities	Failure to manage the talent pipeline or deal with poor performers	Institutional skills developed as required to execute strategy	Distinctive capabilities nurtured to create long-term competitive advantage
Motivation	Low engagement accepted as norm	Motivation promoted through incentives, opportunities, and values	Extraordinary effort generated through employees' sense of meaning and identity
External orientation	Energy of organization directed inward	Primary objective to create value for customers	Focus on creating value for all stakeholders
Innovation and learning	No structured approaches to harnessing employees' ideas	Ideas captured and converted into value incrementally and through special initiatives	Internal and external networks leveraged to maintain leadership position

Bob's Story About Return On Situational Awareness

I will never forget the first time I met Bob. The year was 2008. Bob, CEO of a medium-sized incentive and marketing organization in Ohio, was in his third year in that role.

He shared with me a recent incident.

John, his CFO, closed the door to Bob's office. John was a man not prone to humor.

"Bob, I'm glad you are sitting down because once I share this information," began John, "you may want to punch something, and I don't want to be standing near you."

Bob had been an athlete in high school and college, and his six-foot-three-inch frame created a strong presence.

Bob had been recruited by the board of angel investors because of his ability to find the silver lining in any situation and was someone who would grow the business such that their investment would be repaid in full within five years.

The company had been in business for six years and had recruited a seasoned and high performing group of business development leaders who had created an enviable pipeline of marquee companies across many industries. The board knew it needed to recruit a CEO these talented leaders would respect and one who would complement their relationships and efforts.

Bob is charismatic, affable, resourceful, and strategic. His frequent flyer miles quadrupled as he crossed the country, meeting prospects and existing clients and building solid relationships with his business development leaders.

At the same time, he was identifying the gaps in his team at headquarters, and when he knew he needed a key role to be filled by a new candidate, he followed through. One of the key roles he filled was the CFO. Bob recognized his strengths were about ideas and relationships. He needed a CFO who focused on financial analysis and systems that improve efficiency and accountability.

John, the new CFO, did his homework in his first ninety days. Upon Bob's return from a particularly successful incentive trip with one of the key clients, he asked Bob to clear his calendar for a two-hour meeting to share his findings.

That led to the day John closed the door.

Bob gulped and confidently replied, "I'm ready for your assessment. I'm sure we will have an answer or solutions to whatever problems you've identified."

Later I would discover that was signature Bob, a glass-half-full outlook.

John started out by telling Bob the schedule for repaying the angel investors was off by two years. The goal to go public or be acquired would need to be postponed indefinitely, and that was presuming no unanticipated black swan event (unexpected and having a negative impact) affected their business. The rest of the meeting was sobering and affected Bob's normal upbeat outlook. He sat quietly for the rest of the day, trying to sort out how he was going to turn around this situation. This meeting took place in March 2008.

A senior executive at one of their top clients called the next day to get Bob's recommendation on some new plans. On a hunch, Bob asked him if he knew of a savvy coach/consultant who was good at facilitating strategic thinking and business transformations conversations. The client recommended me.

At my first meeting with Bob, he alternated between being confident and looking like he was going to be punished for not handling things well. He wanted to share the information before I met John, a born worrier, so I would know he was not giving up.

When I meet a client facing this type of dilemma, I am mindful of being more of an observer so I gain full situational awareness. Creating insight in a client gives them confidence they do have key knowledge that will help in the turnaround, yet plants the seed that they will resolve the situation in a timely manner with an experienced and objective performance partner in their corner.

Clearly, Bob's challenges required he transform himself from a cheerleader and innovator for the business to an integrative leader who paid particular attention to extreme situational awareness for the business, industry, and necessary ingredients for thriving in the current business climate. A comprehensive analysis that defined where the business was, and the ecosystem that would contribute to the success of the existing or reframed model, was the first step.

Bob's voice normally did not quiver. However, at the end of this meeting, it did.

"If I commit to the process for mastering this situational awareness step, will we be positioned for an acquisition? A profitable IPO? Will the pioneers who built what we have get a solid return?"

"Absolutely," I replied without hesitation. "Although it won't be easy, you won't be alone because you have successful players who will share the journey with you to create a highly coherent organization."

He laughed and said, "I need to think about how Adam and Chuck will react to the changes that will be required of them." Chuck and Adam were his rainmakers who had established conditions for how they ran their domains.

"Bob, they are resourceful and have business savvy. Let us have an executive offsite that allows them to go through the same 'aha' experience you had during our meeting."

Bob's senior leadership team (SLT) participated in two offsites in 2008. In the first one, (in May 2008) we completed the internal and external audits. Key gaps and opportunities were identified in regard to profitability from each client and membership in the SLT; both were unresolved issues within the organization that affected trust and collaboration.

The offsite uncovered blind spots regarding the return by each client. It was uncomfortable to admit that certain clients that received VIP treatment had not contributed to profitable results. The SLT started to evaluate all client relationships and needs differently. They found out some clients would gladly pay for the extra attention and service. This helped them design new price options, staff appropriately, and improve their efficiency.

We had our next offsite meeting in September 2008. The right steps had been taken in between meetings that ensured those who participated in the second session were committed to the required changes, constructively curious, and focused on building coherence for the leadership team and the company. The focus became where we wanted and needed to be to achieve our two- and five-year goals.

In 2010, the angel investors were paid in full. In September 2012, the organization was acquired by a multibillion-dollar international organization that wanted a US presence in the company's market. The entire leadership team was paid one-year retention bonuses. Bob remained with the organization for two years as senior executive lead for the US and a global executive lead member (top fifty in the organization).

The process and team in place in the fall of 2008 were well equipped with the navigation tools needed to travel the rapids the organization would face on its journey to financial independence.

Aftermath

Bob retired early; however, he did not stay retired for long. On May 1, 2017, Bob collaborated with a private investor group and reacquired the US and Canada division. Today, he is the CEO of a 700-employee organization that is four times the size of the organization he sold in 2012.

Evidence Of Bob's Organization Achieving Elite Health Status

The table shared from the *McKinsey Quarterly* shows Bob's leadership for assessing where the organization was in 2008 resulted in elite results in the years leading to 2012 across all points, but in particular:

- **Direction:** Sense of purpose and engagement about the vision

- **Leadership:** Stretch goals to work at full potential

- **Capabilities:** Distinctive abilities nurtured to create long-term competitive advantage

- **Motivation:** Extraordinary effort generated through employees' sense of meaning and identity

- **Accountability:** "Ownership" mindset encouraged at all levels

Integrative leaders start the journey to organizational coherence by courageously recognizing where they are and where they want to be to achieve success. Return on situational awareness is a journey best shared by membership in a great team. The leader lays the foundation for that team to have a meaningful and rewarding experience.

People often refer to that time in their life as being part of something larger than themselves, of being connected, cohesive. Peter Senge, the author of *The Fifth Discipline*, shares that, "some spend the rest of their lives looking for ways to recapture that spirit."[7] The new firm has four of the original members of the SLT, and Bob is still the captain renewing the spirit.

---

[7] Peter M. Senge, *The Fifth Discipline: the Art and Practice of the Learning Organization* (Doubleday/Currency, 1994).

BECOMING AN INTEGRATIVE LEADER

Conduct an environmental analysis that includes an external and internal audit.

Undertake the external audit from client surveys and industry reports.

Complete an internal audit that includes a SWOT analysis.

Identify key assumptions for where you want to be.

Update your mission and values statements.

Select your top three priority issues.

CHAPTER 4

Optimize Your Return On Investment

R emember the good old days, when your ability to do the four basic math functions—add, subtract, multiply, and divide—was enough to know when you were ahead financially in any transaction?

Now, the interdependencies between different initiatives may cloud the real effect of prior investments for the business. Were we profitable in 2019 because the team became more efficient, or because we reduced our overhead, or took advantage of a local, state or government program? Setting up a sound financial structure that allows for filtering out the effects of different initiatives will inform future decisions.

Business in the twenty-first century needs a new paradigm to generate wealth that sustains an organization. Integrative leaders set priorities and make decisions about resource utilization that will make a profit and provide an advantage to the organization. This step is a left-brain function and is concerned with strategic resource allocation and fiscal strategy. To launch the conversation on the future allocation of resources, questions include:

1. What do we know about the demand?

2. What are our real costs?

3. What is the cost-benefit analysis?

Understanding Return On Investment

Investing in the development of critical thinking skills to understand the business and make complex decisions is critical in C-level roles and provides high-potential bench strength. There are roles, assignments, coaching, and development practices that build business insight and financial acumen, raise decision quality, and build muscle memory for managing complexity. This foundation is at the core of defining the right priorities for the business now.

Return on investment (ROI) is a performance measure on the efficiency of an investment and is one way of relating profits to capital invested. MBA and business majors learn about ROI in their curriculum, yet rarely participate in the conversations that determine and affect ROI in the organization at the start of their careers. It is not uncommon to have a talented leader move up the organization a couple of levels until they reach a role where profit and loss are a component of their compensation. By the time they reach that level, they have been setting priorities for themselves and their teams. Unless they fail miserably, you may never find out if they were the right priorities to provide meaningful ROI. When they meet or exceed goals, the assumption is they managed their resources successfully. What if the tide at the time was lifting all boats? They could have established practices that will harm the organization when the tide is low. Warren Buffett's "when the water (cash/resources) drains, you find out who has been swimming naked" is relevant.

Deliberately mentoring leaders by placing them in roles or assignments where they get a taste of this practice is essential in building a strong bench. A strong coaching/consulting partner with solid tools and business experience will identify the gaps for rounding out the leader's development in mastering the "what" inquiry that reveals ROI opportunities and practices.

Margo's Story About ROI

Margo and I began our coaching program in February 2014. Margo worked at a seventy-year-old Fortune 400 multinational company. During her thirteen years there, she had been promoted laterally into five different positions nationally and internationally, always as finance vice president. Margo was reliable, adaptable (had moved to Germany and the Netherlands with her family), resilient, and a team player with the business and in-country leaders she supported. Margo's career was stalled. She knew she needed to develop additional skills to be promoted. The challenge was identifying those skills.

There was a pattern to her journey. There were always noticeable ROI issues with the areas of the business to which she was assigned. She had proven throughout her career that she could find savings by optimizing distribution, and when appropriate, make solid recommendations to flip processes or business models to deliver the required ROI for the organization. Margo could be counted on to swoop into a sector that was underperforming and work her magic to reset the financials such that the business or sector would contribute to profit. Margo had all the potential to become a transformational global leader, yet her career journey was about being the firefighter. She had accrued solid experience for assessing the crisis at hand. However, firefighters are appreciated in the moment of the crisis, but rarely promoted and developed into a more strategic role.

Raising Margo's profile to senior vice president within the finance function would require that we integrate the skills she had honed in her prior assignments and identify a project with strategic focus where she could put it all together and have an ROI impact on a global level. The organization was expanding into many markets across the world, and the need for a global supply chain function versus a siloed approach became a strategic initiative that year. A new leader with strong global supply chain experience was brought in to oversee those efforts.

The goals we selected centered on complementing her strengths and augmenting her clarity and on-point insights. Integrating her strong financial acumen (left brain) skills with more future-oriented (right brain) skills was the appropriate combination to build strategic agility. Margo would be able to discern future policies, trends, and information that affected the business and the competition. She would be able to create breakthrough strategies and plans. This would now be her brand with a new leader who had no preconceived notions of her capabilities.

Margo's contributions to the supply chain initiative proved invaluable. She had a deep knowledge of the existing systems and where there had been obstacles to optimizing return for the business. She was promoted to SVP of Global Supply Chain in May 2014.

Aftermath

A year later, Margo called me to meet her for lunch. She sounded extremely excited and said, "I need a thought partner who is very practical to explore an opportunity."

During our coaching program, Margo had taken several personality preferences and strengths assessments. She had agreed with the results that indicated she was high energy and driven by reaching for excellence and winning. The exchanges in our coaching had modeled for her how to use her analytic strengths without being "boring" and to exude executive presence.

Margo walked into the restaurant bouncing with a determined gait. "I'm very excited, nervous, and need to look at my situation clearly."

"Okay, I'm all ears. What's going on?"

"I've been approached by a company in the top ten of the Fortune 500. I am a CFO candidate for their international consumer business," she said with a broad smile.

"Wow, that is exciting news!" I replied enthusiastically.

The career of a successful leader has pivotal inflection points: the right role at the right time in the journey of the company and the executive. Key factors in determining success in senior roles when transferring into a new culture and/or industry are much about aligning strengths and critical problems and hurdles the organization is facing. The more I learned about the role, it was clear that Margo would be a strong asset for them. She was naturally curious and nimble in execution.

My only question when I realized there was a good chance she would be selected was, "Have you groomed a successor?"

She smiled in her impish way. "I don't forget the lessons shared. Yes, I do have a candidate in mind."

It was not an easy interview process. It was designed to weed out those who would not fit into the pace and expectations of the organization. This brought out the best in Margo. She enjoys a good challenge.

She became the CFO for their international consumer business in late 2015. Within two years, she was promoted to CFO of worldwide operations. She is definitely thinking and being *big*.

Research Validates

In June 2004, the *Harvard Business Review* reprinted Peter Drucker's recommendation on the practices of "What Makes an Effective Executive."[8] Drucker's practical knowledge is the result of sixty-five years of consulting experience with some of the best business and non-profit CEOs. The first two questions they most ask themselves to give them the knowledge they need to do an effective job are: "What needs to be done?" and "What is right for the enterprise?" He elaborates that effective executives select at most two key objectives. Those objectives are urgent, vital, and communicate the priorities to the rest of the organization.

The business environment has become more complex due to the unlimited range of possible choices to grow, retool, or redefine the arena. The discipline required to secure a solid return on investment demands that everyone in the organization is committed to achieving and/or exceeding the return identified for that market segment. Financially agile teams track results and

---

[8] Peter Drucker, "What Makes an Effective Executive?," *Harvard Business Review*, June 2004.

unexpected turns that move the quarterly and yearly results up or down such that they are not blindsided or can leverage an unexpected opportunity.

BECOMING AN INTEGRATIVE LEADER

Identify competencies to build ROI skills in your organization.

Develop ROI competencies in high potential leaders early in their career.

Identify or create emerging roles where those skills will be practiced under the mentoring of a seasoned leader.

Engage an experienced executive coach to fill in the gaps through a development plan.

CHAPTER 5

Optimize Your Return On Imaginative Intelligence

f I was to ask you about the person who taught you the importance of why you do something, who comes to mind?

For me, it was my business strategy professor in my junior year at the University of Denver. Everyone was afraid to be in his class because he did not suffer fools gladly and had designed the course in an unorthodox way. Unorthodox, in this case, meant highly experiential.

For the entire semester, we were paired up in groups to simulate being in different companies and competing with other companies in our field. To us, success was passing the course; to the professor, it was producing profitable results that confirmed your company's idea and execution were successful in the marketplace. To this day, I remember the tools he shared. At the top of that list is knowing why you are in business.

Meaning, purpose, and reason for what we are doing or inventing are at the core of this step in the journey of an integrative leader. The impetus for seeking this answer may start with an emotion or sense that something is right or wrong. The key to solving this piece of the puzzle requires exploring new neural pathways in our right brain. The return on ideas is correlated to your ability or the ability of the organization to journey often into "possibility thinking."

Innovation is key to many industries, but it is essential in the technology and entertainment examples shared in this chapter. Today, those industries are an integrated model that has adapted to consistent experimentation on both the technology and entertainment sides of the business. The leaders who thrive are full of curiosity and comfortable breaking rules and taking risks. Navigating a successful career while immersed in this energy is all about imaginative intelligence.

Understanding Return On Imaginative Intelligence

Nurturing and developing comfort with ambiguity and innovation management builds this skill set to navigate uncertain times and unexpected opportunities. There is a paradox in the business world to master this practice:

- Certitude creates limits

- Ambiguity provides flexibility and expansiveness

- Breakthrough business success in any sector will depend on adaptability, anticipation, and innovation

Andy Grove, the founder of Intel, was known for identifying, investing in, and thriving on strategic *inflection points* in an industry. When fundamentals are about to change, something is ending, and something new is emerging. In Grove's day, the concern was about the materials and process innovation for creating faster and more dynamic chips. He purposely selected different groups to work on different generations of chips so they would not be blocked by the limitations of the prior group. Grove understood that visionaries do best when there is a clean canvas. Today, the expense and number of resources to dedicate to that effort would be considered a luxury. Intel's reason for being in the business was breakthrough chip technology delivered to the marketplace every six to twelve months. Dominance in that market led to a cascade of revenue streams.

An organization where those who are innovative by nature partner with those who understand that maintaining the status quo leads to obsolesce has the best chance of defining why they are in the business and thriving in the twenty-first century.

Jason's Story About Return On Imaginative Intelligence

The year I met Jason, we were at an after-work business social at a restaurant and bar known for its comfort food. The ratio of coaches to clients was one to four. At this particular company, the organization development team experimented with new ways to create connections between executives who are participating in their leading-edge program and their assigned coaches. They had paired the coaches to the leaders based on their in-depth knowledge of both parties.

The leaders who were participating in this coaching program already had at least two offsites together, so they all knew one another. Everyone had a nametag, and the executives had been given their coach's name while the coaches had been given their executive's name.

The event was designed for introductions to connect a name with a face. Coaches were welcome to stay after the first hour. The leaders knew once the introductions were over, they could fill their plates and sit down with their colleagues for a substantive and fun conversation while partaking in the messy and delicious finger food.

I noticed one group of leaders, two men and two women, in deep discussion. One of the men was more casually dressed and seemed to be thoroughly enjoying the conversation. He was the only one holding an empty appetizer plate.

Awkwardly, I glanced at his nametag while not interrupting the energy in the group.

His large blue eyes darted my way. "Hi, I'm Jason. Are you Sonia?"

"Yes, but please continue with your conversation. We can catch up later."

His colleagues looked my way, and in a chorus, chimed in, "This conversation is ongoing. Jason always adds something new, so it's never done."

Jason moved toward me and invited me to follow him to the appetizer table. "The food is really good. Not many are eating, which gives us the first choice at everything."

It is refreshing to meet someone who is so comfortable in their own skin that deviating from the crowd makes the experience fun and interesting.

Jason was born "down under," and maybe that qualifies him as seeing the world from a different point of view. Jason grew up in entertainment. When he was in Australia as a young man, he was moved to on-air talent on television due to his ability to quickly respond to whatever was going on in the studio and in front of the camera (and also his blond good looks). His energy is all about being nimble. Everything about him moves in a light way, but the most agile part of him is his mind. Jason is the ultimate *dot connector*—not only to what is happening, but to what is possible.

Jason was an emerging leader in the flagship property of a Fortune 5 company. The organization had recognized the value of investing in the next generation of leaders and had put together a program to give the organization a pool of leaders to select as the business grew either by transformation or acquisition. Coaching a leader in these circumstances creates an unlimited potential for magic to happen. The leader is in a focused period for learning and exploring new leadership concepts.

"I'm looking forward to the coaching portion of the program. I hear the conversations are customizable to what I need," Jason shared in a sincere tone.

"That's correct. I'll be more of a thought partner and resource for coming up with a development plan that complements your strengths and provides tools for the areas of weakness," I replied in my soothing coaching tone.

"You mean a plan to address my gaps? I have plenty of them." Jason was self-deprecating, but in a fun way.

That evening, I learned Jason was in love with actionable ideas. He fostered more conversation and diverse thoughts because he wanted to make the most of all the energy he had to innovate.

A leader like Jason appreciates feedback from a 360-process, but needs to translate those experiences and impressions from others to understand why he may not get the support he needs at a critical moment. Leaders with imaginative intelligence often lose their audience, particularly if the audience is anchored in traditional business models that inoculate them from taking risks.

Jason's world was all about what was possible. A multibillion-dollar organization needs to manage many business models. Approval for innovation requires a large return on the concept, or more realistically, a tangible return in the short term. A large return on the concept moves the organization into a new market it can dominate in short order.

Jason's radar needed some tweaking. He needed to create sensors for adjusting his tendency to operate at ninety-miles-per-hour for comfort with ambiguity to a more balanced fifty-five-miles-per-hour to connect with those he needed on board. He also needed to build a supporting constituency for the innovation management process by demonstrating the plans and operations for the innovative ideas he proposed. Validation of this step by others allows for leading or engineering the creative process with them.

Great entrepreneurs are resourceful, which comes in handy when resources are limited. They are passionate about the project, and this energy is contagious. New alliances get on board to support the vision. In times of change, they scale up or down well because they are nimble.

Within three months of our work together, a senior leader in the organization found that Jason's contributions in brainstorming sessions often provided him with new currency with his boss. He was moved into a leadership position reporting directly to this senior leader and given more opportunity to explore his ideas.

Although the area he was responsible for is not the largest, Jason took great pride in making it the most profitable for return on imaginative intelligence. He was thrifty with the budget allocated and exceeded the benchmark provided for profit on that business model. The industry was undergoing a transformation, which meant layoffs and growth through acquisition. The team was lean and empowered. There were no issues in recruiting into his area as the buzz in the organization was that working in this group, you could make a difference. Passion and creativity were the fuel that fed this group to keep performing at a high level because they never knew what interesting project they might work on tomorrow.

Aftermath

In the past two years, the organization acquired an exceptionally large former competitor. In a break from tradition, the organization evaluated the whole talent pool to ensure the cross-pollination would move those ready into the right roles regardless of which side of the acquisition they were on. In Jason's view, that means he has new colleagues he does not know very well. He knows this alters the dynamics for some, but he sees this change as creating unlimited new opportunities. It is like opening up new presents on Christmas morning. True to form, he recently shared that these new circumstances have moved him to brainstorm eight new options for what is possible now. Jason starts from the premise that to be in the business, you need to be best in the category, or offer a new direction that will leverage other organization assets or build a new franchise. Those are goals worth pursuing to be in the market. He is already at work on a transformative model that involves a new division that has complementary properties. He knows his prior contacts who are good at developing the new will inspire the new division to explore how to be best in the category in this new frontier.

Research Validates

The September 2003 issue of *Inc.* magazine featured Robert Redford on the cover with the headline, "How Creativity Drives Profit, The Sundance Model Can Transform Your Business."[9] Redford is an actor, director, producer, and businessman who epitomizes imaginative intelligence. Stephen Zades, the author of the article, is accustomed to business interviews with more traditional CEOs in a more buttoned-up setting. He spent two days following Redford at Sundance to different meetings for upcoming projects. He was

---

9 Stephen Zades, "How Creativity Drives Profit, The Sundance Model Can Transform Your Business.," *Inc.*, September 2003.

surprised there was not one time he repeated himself. Every situation brought up something different in how Redford could contribute or move the process along.

"'Do you think the world was created by an accountant?' Redford asks me. 'No! The universe was created by combustion of a creative explosion fire, and chaos started everything. Then order came on top of that.' Redford explains his philosophy as, 'You had to think not only of revenue but the quality of that revenue.'"

Imaginative intelligence is the ability to convert the raw material of experience and insight across disciplines of knowledge into inventive work. The Sundance Film Festival and Institute are synonymous with building bench strength in the creative arts.

Ed Catmull, president of Pixar Animation Studios and Walt Disney Animation Studios, captured the roller coaster ride involved in pursuing true inspiration and building the culture to sustain that quest in his book, *Creativity, Inc.*[10] Catmull's background as an engineer did not prepare him for what he would learn working with Steve Jobs on how to design and leverage creative know-how into financial results that would make an organization like Disney pay for the return on ideas generated at Pixar Animation. Jobs knew Disney would eventually want to purchase Pixar once it understood how much money it was spending as Pixar's biggest client. Jobs launched the IPO before Disney got the idea. When Disney acquired Pixar, Catmull and Jobs

---

[10] Ed Catmull, *Creativity, Inc* (Random House, 2014).

had more than recouped their investment of time and ideas. In summary, every organization that changes the state of play did so by successfully answering, "Why are we in this business?"

BECOMING AN INTEGRATIVE LEADER

Survey the leader and the direct-reports of each of your groups or divisions on why they are in the business. Correlate this to the financial results and future plans.

Assess the competencies in the associated fields that create imaginative intelligence.

Design a program with organization development or an experienced coach/consultant to enhance the skill set for comfort with ambiguity and innovation management.

CHAPTER 6

Optimize Your Return On Implementation

M arilyn was a smart, tough, but fair head of HR for a major studio. Negotiations with the union looked to be at an impasse. But then the conversations shifted to "how" questions. How would this be implemented? How would this be communicated to the rank and file? How would this be phased in?

Ah, thought Marilyn, *we have reached the resolution stage turning point.*

At that point, the group responsible pivoted to the engineers and implementers. The focus shifted to understanding the altered circumstances so everyone could get back to work.

To get things done, integrative leaders master operational skills. Operations transform *resource* or *data* inputs into desired *goods*, *services*, or *results*. A leader immersed in this step *creates* and delivers strategic thinking for processes that provide value to the customer.

This is a left-brain competency that tends to be the domain of those who are trained as engineers and project managers. They will drill down to understand not only how to make the widget, watch, or drawing, but in the process, streamline the steps to create a return on the implementation. Plans always involve a budget and a timeframe. We consider the project successful when it is delivered within budget and as scheduled. The reason for launching a project is connected to expanded capabilities and/or driving down costs. The return on implementation occurs when the organization begins to experience the benefits the project envisioned.

These leaders get an undeserved branding for fixation with details, adherence to the chain of command, and need for control systems for accountability. However, their work is important and serious because so much rides on their ability to deliver flawless implementations. Their ability to scale the effectiveness of their function is easily measured in the savings they produce. A great idea with ineffective planning and processes loses its impact and will show up with missed bottom-line results. Alternatively, a good idea with mature processes can deliver higher-than-expected profits.

Understanding Return On Implementation

Investing in key operation skills like organizing, planning, and managing work processes establishes a strong foundation for leaders working in any industry. The example in this chapter focuses on information technology, governance structures, engineering, and systems.

C-level leaders know transformations that affect processes contribute to the organization's ability to compete and surpass others in its field. A model to use to assess return on implementation comes from Michael Hammer, a former computer science professor at MIT, who led the practice of business process re-engineering.

Hammer established a new framework by which an organization could conduct a process audit. This audit assessed the process and enterprise maturity model. An organization's process model demonstrates maturity when it is capable of delivering higher performance over time. There are five process enablers and four enterprise capabilities. Using Hammer's model, the owner-leader (a senior executive who has the responsibility for the process and its results) in their function can identify the current process stage to create a meaningful development plan that will grow their skill set to transform operations. See more about the model in the section on *Research Validates*.

Diane's Story About Return On Implementation

Even for a can-do woman like Diane, aerospace is a man's world. Information technology roles in an aerospace and defense organization have not traditionally gone to women, especially when she started her career in 1982.

In the early 1990s, STEM (science, technology, engineering, and mathematics) initiatives were created to attract more women into these fields. However, Diane launched her career at a Fortune 100 aerospace and defense firm a decade before the STEM initiatives. Diane was a pioneer. Pioneers learn early that they will stand out because they are not the norm. There is an inherent double-edged sword to this. All your successes are visible, but so are your mistakes. Conclusions about your potential are sometimes made without you being aware or having the ability to influence them. I met Diane when the organization wanted to invest in the leaders who would be driving change in operations. Diane was the director of information systems technology.

Diane enjoyed her work and liked a challenge. She had different mentors and managers who provided her with strong themes on "what works in this organization." Meetings among subject matter experts with strong credentials for working on complex, multiyear projects required patience and nuance—patience to understand the backstory about the project and nuance in offering suggestions for course corrections.

It got more complex when her department supported both commercial engineering operations and top-secret or "black" programs.

The change initiatives in 2010 required both groups to participate in new processes jointly, something they had never done before. Gaining the support of all parties required that Diane become an effective teacher/practitioner of a not-welcome policy.

The tension created when transparency practices (for those unaccustomed to that approach outside of their select group) and attention to detail practices meet soon dissolves when it is clear this leads to better decisions and implementation. Traditionally, there is tension between commercial and black programs. Black programs are accustomed to operating with others strictly on a need-to-know basis. A brainstorming conversation can devolve into questions that yield curt and unsatisfactory answers for sharing information. You need collaboration on defining what is important to how the final product gets built.

Diane has an infectious laugh and busy blue eyes. She asked me, "You really think I will be successful in transforming the information technology leadership team this year?"

"Diane, you alone can't transform the team such that they support the organization and governance structure changes," I said. "But you can be the catalyst who facilitates the planning and best practice operational initiatives."

This was a new role for Diane. She was used to the "tell" model versus the "ask" model, particularly when the tide was on her side. The operational initiatives were a must-have for future business with the current client base. Her mentors had taught her that the "tell" model was what worked here. This meant she dictated the terms and conditions. On the other hand, the "ask" model required socializing the concepts for the new operation process. It is an inclusive approach to get all on board. It would necessitate flexibility to make course corrections based on knowledge gained in peeling back the existing layers.

"Getting others to contemplate and implement new structures and work processes will succeed when those most affected have a seat at the table for how we all get the work done," I added.

Diane is a "get it done" kind of person. She moved quickly to create an environment that allowed for discussion and critical thinking around transforming processes. Leaning on the process audit model gave this engineering group something to evaluate and reach for. There were a few bumps on the road as the black project group was not sure what it was gaining by sharing the big picture of what it needed to be successful.

Two months into the process, at our next meeting, I asked, "Anything new or different you would like to share?"

"Yes! It's fun being a catalyst. I have learned more about the steps and workarounds the groups have used to keep their head above water supporting the old systems. We all breathed a collective sigh of relief at the last meeting when we agreed to engineer the system that best supports the business and the department. We think besides the cost savings, we will realize efficiencies that mean we will find time to complete special projects that have been in our 'nice to do' backlog."

"Now that's progress," I said. "The team is moving up a level in the process maturity model, and because it's linked to the enterprise model, it's a win-win!"

This was the biggest and most complex project Diane had signed on to in her thirty-year career in the industry. It would have been easy for her to stick to old mental models for how to implement new systems. Instead, she chose a new process for inviting the collective group's wisdom and scars for making the necessary changes.

During our work together, Diane shared some insights she was gaining in leading this transformation project. Here they are in her own words:

- A leader in this type of project provides the drumbeat (sets the tone) for the speed and intensity needed at the different stages.

- A leader pays attention to the small stuff because one member with a different agenda can derail the direction and success of the project. The larger the group, the better a hierarchical structure helps to keep the communication and understanding flowing.

- Teams need to be coached to stay in an *abundance* mentality for the resources that will allow for the completion of the project. (This is particularly important when the organization is cost-cutting.)

- Strategy should match the work in the project. It is the way all those working on the project understand their value and purpose in completing the project. They will work their heads off. This changes the feeling for implementing the work.

This information technology group supports a business exploring new frontiers in space. It raised its level of performance to be better partners with each other and the client. It co-created an integrated and next-level process to generate a solid return on new system implementation. Ready for liftoff, anyone?

Aftermath

Diane served in her new role as information technology director until 2013. She retired with her husband, and they have spent the last six years traveling to new locations, visiting her grandchildren, and serving on boards and committees in her community.

Research Validates

The April 2007 edition of the *Harvard Business Review*[11] featured the process and enterprise maturity model from Hammer. He encouraged organizations to conduct a process audit to identify how they can update and upgrade process to deliver at a high-performance level.

The Process And Enterprise Maturity Model

Companies need to ensure their business processes become more mature—in other words, they are capable of delivering higher performance over time. To make that happen, companies must develop two kinds of characteristics: *process enablers,* which pertain to individual processes, and *enterprise capabilities,* which apply to entire organizations.

Five Process Enablers

Design: The comprehensiveness of the specification of how the process is to be executed

---

[11] Michael Hammer, "The Process Audit," *Harvard Business Review*, April 2007.

Performers: The people who execute the process, particularly in terms of their skills and knowledge

Owner: A senior executive who has responsibility for the process and its results

Infrastructure: Information and management systems that support the process

Metrics: The measures the company uses to track the process's performance

Four Enterprise Capabilities

Leadership: Senior executives who support the creation of processes

Culture: The values of customer focus, teamwork, personal accountability, and a willingness to change

Expertise: Skills in, and methodology for, process redesign

Governance: Mechanisms for managing complex projects and change initiatives

Companies can use their evaluations of the enablers and capabilities, in tandem, to plan and assess the progress of process-based transformations.

BECOMING AN INTEGRATIVE LEADER

Conduct a yearly survey on the key operational skills for process implementation and improvement in your organization.

Use the results of this survey to identify two areas for improvement for the upcoming year across your division and/or department.

Select meaningful metrics for assessing return on implementation of your work process.

Conduct a process audit prior to any significant implementation changes for your product or service business.

CHAPTER 7

Optimize Your Return On Interpersonal Interaction

Would it surprise you to know that surgeons who have a good bedside manner are less likely to be sued?

Yes, it is true. An emotional intelligence expert shared with me that doctors and other attending medical professionals involved in surgeries in which there is a problem for the patient are less likely to be sued when they have an emotionally intelligent bedside manner.

She explained to me it was because the patient has established a positive emotional connection. This relationship makes it harder to want to hurt or damage someone with whom we have empathy. My sister, who was the in vitro fertilization director at Johns Hopkins Hospital, confirmed this.

Integrative leaders have a keen awareness of their interpersonal skills and their effect on others. They understand that in addition to running the "hard" side of the business, they also lead the "soft" social system of their business, which shapes the way people work together.

The ability to get at the truth of someone before they join your organization, or who may already be part of the company, requires practicing and mastering right-brain skills. The good news is our brain and internal chemistry are wired to connect.

The field of emotional intelligence launched in 1994 when Daniel Goleman published his first book on the subject. Twenty-six years later, many books, assessments, and organizational development leaders have focused on the challenges and opportunities for honing in on the soft skills of leading. The competencies required for capable leadership in this area fall into three areas: building collaborative relationships, optimizing diverse talent, and influencing others. Exit interviews have revealed that people join a *company* but often leave because of a *manager* or *team* mismatch. This represents an emotional intelligence failure.

The journey for weathering a crisis, seizing opportunities, and delivering outstanding results in the marketplace requires a solid team of colleagues whose work together is greater than the sum of their individual parts. The recipe for success in this area is a blend of chemistry (willingness to understand others), attitude (positivity and goodwill), and living rules of engagement for teamwork (what works here).

Understanding Return On Interpersonal Interaction

In his book, *Emotionomics,*[12] Dan Hill analyzes the role of emotions in consumer and employee behavior. It is no mystery that a large component of our decision-making process for the products we purchase, the people we hire, and the organizations we support are our feelings about them.

In my coaching practice, there is a consistent phrase I share with the leaders: "People never forget how you made them feel." If you want them to feel differently about you, you have to change your mindset and behavior.

Investing in the tools and interactions that build the competency for people management is critical to any organization. The returns on building collaborative relationships are realized when constructive conflict conversations lead to airing out different points of view. What remains is the best option for solving the problem. Building networks up, down, and across the organization instills a partnership orientation and breaks down current and future obstacles.

The return on optimizing diverse talent happens when you and your leaders attract and develop top talent

---

[12] Dan Hill, *Emotionomics: Leveraging Emotions for Business Success* (London: Kogan Page, 2008).

infused with emotional intelligence. They become the cornerstone for building highly effective teams. Diversity and inclusion have become a department in human resources, which started as an initiative from the C-Suite. Valuing the differences in thought and experiences lays the foundation for exploring new options to success for the business.

The return on influencing people is essential in today's multicultural market and workplace. Organizational savvy and effective communication are pillars for being persuasive. You cannot drive vision and purpose with low engagement skills.

A good example of someone who has mastered the influencing skills competency comes from a C-level executive who shared the following strategies he uses when he is working with others who have the power to disagree:

- Listen and reflect; you may hear things differently or find common ground

- Look for an indirect approach that would help them understand your point of view without rejecting it outright

- Switch and reframe to their position (choose your battles)

- Propose a compromise

- Exert influence on others who you know are influential to their point of view

- Accept that you are wrong

Catherine's Story About Return On Personal Interaction

If you were wrongfully accused of a crime, you would want Catherine to be foreman of the jury evaluating your case. Catherine has a great "BS detector." She carefully evaluates all the information provided and inquires about the relevant information that is not volunteered. She is a good observer, which strengthens her ability to read the room to understand where others stand on an issue.

I met Catherine at one of the big-five American film studios that has a ninety-year history for making quality content. Although the organization has been acquired by two other communication companies in the past ten years, it still enjoys a strong reputation for being a talent-friendly studio.

Nine months before we met, Catherine had been promoted to executive vice president and general manager for technology solutions and technical operations. Information technology plays a critical role in the support and delivery of the products and services to the marketplace.

The year was 2015, and the challenge ahead for the organization was to bring all technology-related teams and departments under one umbrella. In an effort to not be disruptive, but evolutionary, it was agreed there would be a two-year phased-in approach to standing up the new organization.

For Catherine to successfully stand up the new organization would require strong interpersonal skills and tools for growing relationships and alliances across the studio. Catherine's focus within the IT department was the successful integration of all segments contained within the two major information technology groups. One group was led by Catherine and the other by another leader who had been with the organization for decades. The cross-pollination of skills and leadership would be a major benefit to the organization. Catherine and her supervisor wanted an organizational transformation with minimum factionalism disrupting the journey.

When selecting me to be her coach, Catherine asked the critical question toward the end of the meeting: "Which one of the female presidents in the organization has a leadership style and philosophy that builds coherence during and after a transformation? Should I be patterning myself after her?"

I could feel myself reviewing the faces and culture of each of the women-led groups before sharing my answer. Catherine clearly appreciated that I was thoughtful before responding. "You will need to forge the way. None of them have had to integrate the entire studio capabilities to support all the current and future businesses."

She replied, "Thank you for being honest. I appreciate your candor. I will need your unvarnished feedback to navigate the rapids and obstacles ahead. Now I know I can count on you."

"I look forward to our work together. It helps that you know it will not be easy, and more importantly, has never been done here. That creates the possibility for a lot of second-guessing by others, but we will have a plan for that eventuality, too," I replied.

The best way to learn about the brand you have cultivated as a leader are the results of a 360-evaluation. My advice in selecting the raters is a balance of your fans and critics. I am always pleasantly surprised when the best advice comes from the critics. They tend to be clearer about what they do not understand or perceive that upsets them. Catherine was courageous and put together a comprehensive list of information technology experts across the businesses and thought leaders across the organization. This survey provided information that was the foundation for her development plan in 2016.

We learned Catherine was an enigma to the IT organization she did not lead. Any impressions they had of Catherine's preferences and priorities came either from water cooler conversations or announcements from her group without context. When others don't know much, they fill in the white space with impressions or second- or third-hand stories. There was also a legacy notion that the side she led had all the fun and attention because they "got to do innovation."

Catherine was a quick study, even in areas that were outside her comfort zone. She was not prone to draw attention to herself; her preference was to feature her team, the data, and the project results. She worked for an entertainment company that was accustomed to charismatic and big presence leaders. After all, they deal with on-camera talent who is practiced at holding an audience.

In the beginning, Catherine began to hold small townhall meetings to share the vision and gave anyone attending the opportunity to express what was top of mind for them. Experiencing Catherine's thoughtful approach and openness to new ideas on how the new organization should be designed created the right chatter for embracing the changes ahead. It's hard to resist a caring, transparent leader who listens and who ensures the right decisions are made for the well-being of both the team and the organization.

She ventured into new waters by building new and stronger relationships with studio leaders. The more she understood their challenges, the more options she could share about what technology solutions were available to address them.

In the midst of all this change, Catherine had the opportunity to spend time on innovation management, a clear strength and passion for her. It is refreshing when the leader navigating the ship to new shores has an affinity for the new horizons. The cross-pollination of ideas and opportunities dispelled the notion that one side had all the fun. The new requirements brought innovation assignments across the entire organization.

No transformation is complete without changes in personnel and teams. These decisions are not easy, but keeping the drama to a minimum was a sign that everyone involved was treated fairly.

My final meeting with Catherine and her supervisor to review progress toward her goals was fun. There was so much good news to share, even though the final part of the journey was still a year away.

Aftermath

Catherine was promoted to chief information officer and chief technology officer in 2017. Her brand today is about creating environments that foster excellence, diversity, and innovation. In her fifteen years at the organization, she has been promoted six times. Every role allowed her to learn more about the contributions each member of her team was capable of delivering as they collectively built a high-performance team. She continues to communicate, influence, and inspire within her function and across the organization.

Research Validates

In May 2018, McKinsey and Co. published an article titled, "Successfully Transitioning to New Leadership Roles."[13] The recommendations from authors Scott Keller and Mary Meany are that organizations deploy the resources needed to help a leader in a new role, particularly a transformational role. Catherine's successful results highlight her attention and plans for delivering in the five dimensions described below: business function, culture, team, yourself, and other stakeholders. Four of the five dimensions deal with who is part of the transformation. Mining, and in some cases, reinventing a leader's interpersonal skills, is at the core of successful transformations. The typical time frame for reinventing how a company or function does business is twenty-two months. At the end of that period, Catherine's results were recognized in her promotion to the CIO and CTO roles.

---

[13] Scott Keller and Mary Meany, "Successfully Transitioning to New Leadership Roles," McKinsey and Co., May 2018, www.mckinsey.com.

Exhibit 2

Leaders should think about mounting a transition in two equal steps: first take stock, then take action across five dimensions.

Business Function	Culture	Team	Yourself	Other Stakeholders
Take stock: Do you understand the current performance and capabilities? **Take action:** Have you aligned and mobilized your team and organization on future aspirations and priorities?	**Take stock:** Do you understand the current culture and any shifts required to improve performance? **Take action:** Are you influencing those shifts with all levers available?	**Take stock:** Do you have the right team with the right skills and attitudes and structure? **Take action:** Have you together embarked on a structured journey to become a high-performing team?	**Take stock:** Have you done what it takes to get up to speed, set boundaries, and consider your legacy? **Take action:** Do you spend your time wisely by assuming roles only you can play?	**Take stock:** Do you understand your mandate and the other expectations of major stakeholders? **Take action:** Have you established a productive working rhythm and relationship with them to shape their views?

BECOMING AN INTEGRATIVE LEADER

Define an organization competency framework for people leadership.

Build collaborative relationship competency by providing assessments and tools to manage conflict and build interpersonal savvy and networks.

Optimize diverse talent by identifying leaders who value differences, develop talent, and build effective teams.

Develop strong influencing skills by providing assessments and tools for communication effectiveness, driving engagement, and strong persuasion practices.

Provide mentors when onboarding leaders or promoting them to help with navigating formal and informal channels and give context to the organization's culture.

CHAPTER 8

Optimize Your Return On Cognitive Agility

H ave you ever met someone whose superpower is the ability to connect all the dots—the type of person who can view a complex problem and see a critical element that is undetectable to everyone else? Joe, a business affairs attorney for a large entertainment firm, had a boss with that cognitive agility superpower.

Joe and his team had worked on the many details of a global contract their organization was finalizing with an organization whose valuable IP (intellectual property) was important to the company.

The stakes are high when there are loopholes that affect long-term revenue percentages. Joe's team was methodical in its process to avoid a loss or create risk for the organization.

One day before the contract was sent out for signature, his team had taken over a conference room and had all the sections of the contract laid out on the conference table for review by all the attorneys.

Right before lunch, his boss Angela dropped in to share some information with Joe. He was in a conversation with a colleague, giving Angela time to scan the documents.

A few minutes later, Angela asked, "How will you be handling ____?" The detail she was asking about was essential, but due to recent changes in classification by different jurisdictions was particularly complex.

Everyone in the room looked up, startled. Clearly, Angela had honed-in on their blind spot. Their confidence was seeping away about meeting the deadline and having a solid contract. She moved to the whiteboard and laid out two options that could remedy the situation.

If you could see the speed at which they were processing the information, you would have seen smoke coming out the top of their heads. Angela's cognitive agility was evident. Her ability to reconfigure strategy, structure, processes, people, and technology quickly toward value-creating and value-protecting opportunities was instinctive.

Integrative leaders recognize that of all the choices they make to create a profitable and well-run organization, how time is spent and seized is critical. It can mean the difference between leading a category, establishing a strong advantage, or relegating one's business to survival or failure. There is an inherent dilemma baked into when to stop, go, or pause. You need cognitive agility to get it exactly right in any of those circumstances. Solving problems that require accessing different brain competencies builds cognitive agility. The dilemma is, do you rely on your experience of what worked or were best practices, or do you approach this with a beginner's mind?

Eastern philosophy emphasizes that a self-realized master always operates in the present. She or he is not trapped or attached to the past and is not deluded or clouded by the future. The discipline of coming from the beginner's mind connects them to the prevalent zeitgeist. This alignment allows them to tap into their experience toolbox to confirm which door to pursue now. The turnaround for accessing their storehouse of knowledge is shorter for integrative leaders.

The whole brain is involved in evaluating when to take action. The scanning for relevant information from your neural connection networks is complemented by your awareness of the current circumstances. You are zooming in and out, which develops and applies intuition. Good intuition is based on a deep knowledge of a topic.

An example of good intuition in American sports is a baseball player skilled at stealing bases. His experience, instincts, real-time observations, and talent all combine to give him cognitive agility: when to run and when to stay put. The outcome of the game can depend on it. And all those ingredients are necessary for executives whose decisions on timing (new product release, international expansion, entry into a new market, etc.) can make or break a company,

Return On Cognitive Agility

Integrative leaders have an instinct that prepares them to recognize when to put up the sails or stay in port. It is about their learning agility, practice, habits, and experience. Continuously learning new things is the secret to their success.

Organizations knowingly hire for high IQ, as is often the case for graduates with advanced degrees. This means the left-brain competencies for analysis and technical affinity will be practiced instinctively. New behaviors are the currency of high learners. They are skilled at integrating left- and right-brain competencies in various settings.

Preference for left-brain thinking aligns with more deliberate planning and methodical change. The comfortable time horizon is weeks, months, quarters, and years. Right-brain preference is receptive to moving when lightning strikes. A sudden insight where the solution is revealed confirms that acting quickly will yield good results. Investing in a high potential or top talent leader to continuously learn while doing something new will create new neural pathways. The brain becomes ambidextrous, which will yield strong results when faced with complex challenges.

Adaptable leaders thrive whether they are immersed in different geographic locations, varied industry experience, or dissimilar organization size. This high learning agility gives leaders more options for when they should act on a problem or opportunity.

The state of play in business is about transformation and breakthroughs. The market for a product or service can take off or contract in a heartbeat. Learners are keen observers of themselves, others, and situations. The neural pathways for understanding what is going on now are well-traveled no matter the situation. They have more conscious learning tactics they can tap at a moment's notice. They are not afraid of thoughtful experimentation and practice evaluating what worked and did not for every project. Their chances of getting it right increase because they discern what was relevant to a prior success or failure. This often results in their sharing that their well-honed instinct was engaged when they made the right timing call.

Nicholas's Story About Return On Cognitive Agility

I research the background of every leader with whom I have a chemistry meeting. It gives me perspective on what type of communication, focus, and relevant experience to discuss in our meeting. I know they will be meeting or have met at least two other candidates to decide who will be their coach for this engagement.

The profile I had for Nicholas from my research anticipated a no-nonsense leader who would not spend much time on small talk. He is an accomplished engineer who has worked with a successful startup (meaning it went public at a good return to the investors), was a laboratory leader at MIT for Department of Defense programs, and now is a director of engineering for a critical product line used for defense. A director of engineering has both technical and program management responsibilities. It is where all the action is for delivering the products to precise specifications, on time, and within budget.

Two of the walls in his office were decorated with the football paraphernalia of his college team. It so happened it is the same college my brother attended. I was caught unaware and instinctively said, "Go Blue!" Nicholas walked around his desk and greeted me with a smile.

"Have you been to The Big House?" The Big House is what their stadium is called.

We spent a good seven minutes discussing the team's record, their star players who now play professionally, and what the prospects were for them winning the 2014 season. The warmth and sincere passion for his team revealed a personal side to Nick that I perceived had helped him build strong teams during his leadership journey.

Nick seamlessly transitioned into business mode to discuss the current challenges in his new role. This was his first time working at the corporate location while having ultimate responsibility for three remote locations. He wanted a thought partner to challenge him and raise his ability to make the right timing decisions for projects, personnel changes, and dealing with new clients. He was now the newest member of an established leadership team. Building the alliances and trust of that group was paramount to securing the resources his business would need.

The product lines Nick was responsible for operated in different locations and in different company cultures. In the new world, they would be part of each other's supply chain. Coherence was critical to build a way to fit them together in a logical and meaningful way and not take a decade to deliver.

We discussed the different potential variables involved in each area. He has a good poker face, because I was not sure when I walked out of his office whether we would be working together in the future.

Nick is a strong left-brain leader—he is good at "what" and "how" conversations around the operations of the business. His team is technical in nature, so there is a natural understanding of what is top of mind for the engineers and leaders on it. He is comfortable with longer-term horizons for planning and decision-making.

He has ventured into right-brain competencies when technical innovation or personnel changes are required. There is experiential knowledge that has been accrued into his mental database for those matters. What was required now was the integration of all those experiences into a learning model that would provide a backdrop for the new situations he would be facing.

Nick is a practically curious leader. Individuals and leaders who are immersed in complexity appreciate the elegance afforded by simplicity. John Maeda's book, *The Laws of Simplicity,*[14] provided a good tool to intrigue Nick on what a beginner's mindset might look like. Maeda provides ten laws and three keys for simplicity. Nick settled on one law and one key that he could conjure up when he needed to engage the beginner's mind. He chose the tenth law: simplicity is about subtracting the obvious and adding the meaningful. He then chose the third key, power: use less, gain more. Delegating with high trust to empower others on the team was a new practice he needed to master. He would be building intuition around his team competencies.

Nick's ability to quickly reconfigure strategy, structure, processes, people, and technology toward value-creating and value-protecting opportunities would demonstrate cognitive agility. His portfolio included a vintage and formerly profitable product line that needed to engineer a smooth transition to the next generation. He was also dealing with new clients that

---

[14] John Maeda, *The Laws of Simplicity* (Mit Press, 2006).

presented some risk—political, financial, or military. Managing new risks for the organization was much like being an entrepreneur. There was no history to fall back on.

There are many interdependencies an integrative leader needs to fit into the puzzle to arrive at the best timing to launch, terminate, or pause production or an initiative. The plasticity of their learning agility reduces the time spent on the decision.

Nick's 360-feedback provided by his leadership team colleagues in the different product lines was the final piece we needed to identify for building learning, agile teams that would become world-class during the next two years. In doing so, Nicholas and the team would be leveraging return on cognitive agility.

Aftermath

Nick completed the integration of the teams and cultures by the beginning of 2016. He also cultivated solid relationships with his peers such that they would leverage each other's team strengths.

An integrative leader with strong learning agility is open to experiences and alliances that will help them "jump the curve" in new and unexpected challenges. A top internet firm offered Nick a new opportunity to lead a technical program. He joined them for three and a half years.

In 2019, Nick returned to the aerospace firm where I met him in 2014 at two levels above where he left. He is now chief engineer for a $4 billion business segment.

His return on cognitive agility keeps getting stronger. On a personal level, Nick understood that leading a technical project for a leading online firm would prove valuable to his professional experience. The timeframe for delivery on those projects is shorter with a wider user scope. I am not surprised his employer understands that his experience will enhance their leadership ranks.

Research Validates

The *Harvard Business Review* of March 2008[15] focused on assessing whether organizations are a learning organization. The assessment tool is designed to pinpoint areas where a group needs to foster knowledge sharing, idea development, learning from mistakes, and holistic thinking. These would build cognitive agility throughout the function.

The building blocks of the learning organization are:

1. Supportive learning environment

2. Concrete learning processes and practices

3. Leadership that reinforces learning

---

[15] David A. Garvin, Amy C. Edmondson, and Francesca Gino, "Is Yours a Learning Organization," *Harvard Business Review*, March 2008.

There are components within each block to provide actionable intelligence from the assessment. Supportive learning environments provide psychological safety for sharing critical thinking, appreciate different points of view and openness to new ideas, and allow time for reflection.

Concrete learning processes and practices include experimentation, information collection, analysis, education and training, and information transfer.

Leadership that reinforces learning is modeled by inviting others into discussions, asking questions that grow "aha" experiences, model excellent listening skills, and encourage different points of view, which gives the team the experience of speaking truth to power when appropriate.

The goals Nick needed to achieve would be successful by modeling and fostering a learning organization across his divisions.

BECOMING AN INTEGRATIVE LEADER

Identify the learning agility tools and practices used in your organization that build learning at all levels.

Update them to reflect the challenges and opportunities you face now.

Identify roles and projects for your high potentials to experience that will reconfigure strategy, structure, processes, people, and technology quickly toward value-creating and value-protecting opportunities.

Invest in mindfulness training that provides the experience of a beginner's mind.

Create career paths where the integration of prior knowledge and new experiences build leaders, confidence and cognitive agility.

CHAPTER 9

Creating A Culture Of Integrative Leadership

S urprising statistic: The May 2010 *Harvard Business Review* published a survey of top talent leaders that revealed 25 percent of them planned to jump ship within the next year.[16] The survey identified what employers are doing wrong to keep them and made recommendations for changing their minds.

Do you want to keep the top talent in your organization? Identify the riskiest and most challenging positions and place them in these roles with individual development plans. *The Integrative Leader Model* is designed to guide your emerging leaders through the steps and apply skills to meet the challenge or opportunity.

---

[16] Jean Martin and Conrad Schmidt, "How To Keep Your Top Talent," *Harvard Business Review*, May 2010.

How do talented high-performing leaders know they are on the journey to achieving their full potential? We measure performance by the position, compensation, and scope of responsibilities. I propose a model that develops new neural pathways as the leader grows their awareness of how elements are linked within them and within the business. Curious leaders are practiced in asking different questions that often reveal how things are interrelated. This habit raises the option for recognizing a blind spot for themselves or the organization that raises their level of performance.

Many career paths build on a particular discipline or area of expertise. The enhanced focus on collaboration across the organization provides exposure to other areas. The norms for getting at the real issue within the organization determine the level of candor and clarity for building the interconnection database for all who participate.

The choice(s) leaders face when confronting extreme challenges or opportunities are not made in a vacuum. They affect a dynamic and interdependent system that responds in new ways when a shift in pattern and direction occurs. Setting the organizational compass to a True North position in which the leader seeks to understand the big picture leads to organizational coherence.

Integrative leaders acquire the habit and discipline to recognize what is the state of play for the organization by walking around in *The Integrative Leader Model* frequently. Each journey through *The Integrative Leader Model* builds resilience and creates new neural pathways for the brain to engage. They lead the team in the options for a return to achieve their goals.

Understanding Return On Integrative Leadership

There are two questions I ask myself when coaching a leader. How much experience do they have thriving in the midst of change to their industry, organization, and career? And, what lessons and habits have they adopted from the leaders who had the biggest impact on their career?

The average time an individual will be active in the business world before retiring is forty years. Prior to the 2000s, a stable and top-talent leader would be a part of at most four organizations—potentially one for every decade. Today, that number could easily double.

The Integrative Leader Model is designed to help a leader think like Leonardo da Vinci, the quintessential Renaissance thinker, who sought to understand how systems worked, be they human or scientific. His neural connections between right- and left-brain were well-traveled. This is why besides being a gifted artist, he was also an inventor in the fields of engineering and architecture. His works can lead us to conclude that he either achieved his full potential or was remarkably close to it.

The present and future business environments need leaders who navigate complexity well. They will thrive because they have built a large and always growing portfolio and database of mental models connected to real-world experience. They make meaningful connections within and between systems that spark the imagination.

These are **steps in the model** to complement their development plans.

Why we are in this business clears the clutter for engaging a team into possibility thinking. The answer to this determines everything. It is the blueprint for resource allocation and market relevance. It is a strong ingredient for successful reinventions and building demand. This is a key step in mastering the practice of a beginner's mind.

Where we are now sets the compass to the right location for understanding the current state of affairs and dependencies that will affect executing against the plan.

What needs to be done to define the optimal return on investment is a crucial step in the model. This step involves the application of strategic tools for positioning the organization's capabilities within the relevant markets.

How we deliver the full scope of products and services is about tightening up loose ends in the supply chain and tapping into new capabilities because the blueprint from the process audit keeps it fresh and real.

Selecting and developing teams with diverse talent and experience provide the seen and unseen return on interpersonal connections that go the extra mile. An engaged, high-performing team can achieve anything.

Cognitive agility, which synthesizes all the input that comes from both sides of the brain, delivers information on timing in an efficient manner. Timing is everything in catching and riding the right wave. The learning agility quotient is well developed for integrative leaders to recognize that wave. This agility evolves as they experience and master each step in the model.

Merging Engineering Disciplines Story

The backbone of America's economy is the private small business sector. This is the entrepreneur arena. They are tested on many levels. To survive beyond five years, they need to have a product or service that is successful in the marketplace, secure strong clients, ensure financial dexterity, and attract and develop talented employees who provide a solid return to the organization.

In 2013, a partner at a successful mechanical engineering firm in Southern California invited me to a meeting with his new electrical engineer partners, who also had a strong track record of success. The purpose was to engage in an open conversation on the ingredients of high-performing cultures. One of the partners on the electrical side was an avid reader of organizational improvement ideas and practices.

The focus of the meeting was to understand the return on pursuing a coaching culture across the newly formed organization. At that time, they had two offices—a headquarters and a regional office. There were eighty employees who would be learning how to best complement and collaborate on projects with occasionally shared clients.

I was pleasantly surprised that a leader from a strong left-brain discipline was exploring conversations about right-brain and whole-brain topics. I was intrigued that executives who had built strong businesses were willing to contemplate alternate ways of moving forward together. They were focused on building a firm that would outlive their leadership and secure a profitable return to the next generation of leaders.

There have been many initiatives the partner leadership team has undertaken in their desire to build a resilient and sustainable firm. Seven years have passed since those first exploratory conversations. One of the original partners moved on, and two new partners have been developed who manage two of the new offices. (They now have a total of six offices, one out of state.) At their peak employment, they tripled the original eighty colleagues. They have added three new disciplines in their quest to be a full-service engineering partner to the architectural firms they support. It has been a bumpy ride at times, but the core they have built gets stronger because of the trust, engagement, and learning agility they promote.

We have held two leadership meeting summits to arrive at a return on location. They have embraced coaching at the leadership level to ensure new tools and conversations are building new leadership competencies and enhancing the culture.

At a recent digital meeting to review lessons learned in the opening of remote and regional offices, a principal who had been with the firm for a year shared how special it was to have a leadership team willing to give a voice to the next generation of leaders. He knows of what he speaks, as he has worked for three other firms. Resilient and innovative cultures embrace and reward cognitive diversity. They know that understanding what is working and not working is critical to building an organization that will yield a strong future to all concerned.

Research Validates

A *Harvard Business Review* article titled, "How to Keep Your Top Talent" reveals that nearly 40 percent of internal job moves involving high potentials end in failure.[17] If you want to keep your rising stars on track, the following is a summary of what the article revealed.

1. Do not just assume they are engaged. If emerging leaders do not get stimulating work, lots of recognition, and the chance to prosper, they can quickly become disenchanted.

---

[17] Jean Martin and Conrad Schmidt, "How To Keep Your Top Talent," *Harvard Business Review*, May 2010.

2. Do not mistake current high performance for future potential. Stars will have to step up into tougher roles. Explicitly test candidates for three critical attributes: ability, engagement, and aspiration.

3. Do not delegate talent development to line managers. That only limits stars' access to opportunities and encourages hoarding of talent. Manage the quantity and quality of high potentials at the corporate level.

4. Do not shield talent. Place stars in "live fire" roles where new capabilities can—or must—be acquired.

5. Do not assume high potentials will take one for the team. A critical factor determining a rising star's engagement is the sense that he or she is being recognized—primarily through pay. So, offer A-players differentiated compensation and recognition.

6. Do not keep young leaders in the dark. Share future strategies with them—and emphasize their role in making them come to fruition.

BECOMING AN INTEGRATIVE LEADER

Define organization coherence such that leaders tune their compass to True North.

Identify the tough assignments where leaders will develop and test new capabilities.

Build a succession leadership bench that is included in the direction and opportunities for the organization.

Create a return rating tool that measures progress for return on situational awareness, investment, ideas, personal interaction, implementation, and cognitive agility.

Tailor a development plan for integrative leaders with a seasoned coach who will provide the mentoring and partnership to grow situational savvy.

CHAPTER 10

Into The Future Of Integrative Leadership

Based on my twenty-two years as an executive coach, I know one thing is for certain: leaders are faced with extraordinary changes in the decade ahead. Not all leaders are equipped to handle the stress of these uncertain times. However, integrative leaders have the competencies to lead with grace under pressure.

These are the three core competencies of integrative leaders as the business moves forward:

Integrative leaders are a strong asset in the midst of change because they easily engage multiple scenarios and frameworks for dealing with uncertainty. The planning horizon for the six to eighteen months beginning July 1, 2020 can best be defined as ambiguous.

Integrative leaders will innovate to create and meet a new demand for their products or services. They will discern what events and resources are aligning to create openings and flow for the company.

Integrative leaders know we need each other to get through difficult circumstances. Their leadership experience is about the whole being greater than the sum of its parts. They reach out and tap into others' experiences and knowledge to facilitate conversations and planning in many directions with many constituencies.

The Magic Wand Approach

When coaching a leader that I perceive is stuck with old mental models, here is my suggestion. Take out your magic wand and invent the world you would want if you knew you will not fail and were the ultimate authority.

Integrative leaders will play an important role in designing the practices and policies that build resilient organizations. It has already begun as the following vignettes describe.

The learning agility of the leaders whose responsibilities included moving their business or organization to dial down and stabilize in a shutdown of normal operations that lasted months is off the charts. There are many new paradigms they can share that will advance the ability to adapt to a new future. The compressed reaction time frame to move their employees, clients, and stakeholders into a virtual, digital model designed new neural pathways for planning, solving problems, and innovating. Their relation to timing horizons, change in process, and understanding the interdependencies of the options under consideration is operating at a new level. All this learning will now be applied to going back to work—most likely in a quite different state than we remember prior to the shutdown.

At a 2020 roundtable of CIO leaders from different organizations in my county, they shared some of what they experienced. The ability of their teams to be responsive and perform at unimaginable speed was impressive and changed their conversations and expectations. To be relevant and participate in the new economy requires unprecedented knowledge and comfort with digital technology. For cities and educational organizations, it revealed the disparity to digital access and the ability to adapt to this new information and communication forum by 25 percent of their constituents, faculty, and students. Initiatives to balance disparity and intensive sessions with novice users occurred in record time. All who participated now have ambidextrous brain patterns and experiences and are well on their journey to being integrative leaders.

Time For Reinvention

Reinvention is possible when there is an agreement that an existing model or plan is no longer able to deliver the intended results. My vision for the future of business is one where we optimize opportunity and talent to maximize wealth for the many. This requires a change to the traditional path of the industry. For the sake of example, any established industry would work.

When an industry begins, the barrier to entry is low, which invites many to participate. There is an explosion of creativity and experimentation that fosters imaginative intelligence. The products and services are serving different needs and solving known and unforeseen challenges. The path to maturity in most industries is about a reduction in organizations and specialization such that a monopoly or oligarchy of firms emerges. In the past, we have concluded that the firms that survive and become leaders had better products, services, and leadership.

However, there are other factors that play a part in survival. The financial sector is conditioned and incentivized to back those they deem strong and with the access to capital to determine the winners. Resources are redirected to smooth the road for a few companies. Government or regulatory sectors will be influenced by the winners to enact laws in their favor. This often reduces competition and opportunities for others with better or different solutions in the future. The consumer, the ultimate user of the product and service, is not well served in this model. A business environment where integrative leadership is practiced invites conversations about different returns for an organization, market, and industry. How we define success matters. The untapped talent in human beings with a desire to make a difference, solve problems, and experience fulfillment for their contributions would create several strong economies. This was a lesson learned by Bill Hewlett and Dave Packard as HP began to grow. They decentralized promising businesses and often selected new communities in cities close to a college or university to bring on new talent that flourished. The pace of unimaginable growth was sustained because the autonomy translated into ownership for the impact and results each division could deliver.

A society that balances creating opportunities for those available to participate in the workforce with responsibility for building strong and healthy communities welcomes the leadership and vision of integrative leaders. Decentralized options allow for an organic approach to the evolution of an industry and the organizations that will innovate, thrive, and serve all consumers. Integrative leaders are searching for meaningful returns in a variety of areas to optimize the resources and benefit all concerned.

My Vision Comes Full Circle

In a way, my vision comes full circle from what I learned at HP about being a productive and valuable corporate citizen whose participation makes a difference for everyone. HP offered profit-sharing with checks to every employee. It was paid twice a year, in July and December. During the years I worked there, each check was the equivalent of a month's wages. In the summer, it paid for the family vacation, and in the winter, it assured there would be gifts and celebration for the holidays.

HP arrived at its remarkable level of profitability because we were encouraged to find better ways to do things, be accountable for how we used resources (particularly our time), and value contributions from everyone regardless of their level.

I submit that the HP Way encouraged our ability to think differently about our ability, position, contribution, and community. We often engaged in conversations that challenged each other's thinking, so we would be sure the debate led to the best possible option. New neural pathways emerged for everyone. I was fascinated to learn from a colleague who had not participated in one of those sessions that the insights from a meeting had become a key takeaway for him. Knowledge that created "aha" experiences was valued and shared because all who participated knew how it would help others be successful, and in turn, benefit the overall company.

HP was founded during the depression. The founders forged strong partnerships with those who helped them get their business started, including future competitors that provided access to capacities they needed but could not finance. They learned that collaboration in hard times lays the foundation for all to grow and make a bigger pie. Their motivation for launching the company was to design and deliver products that solved complex problems, which also provided a good return to all concerned. They instituted profit-sharing in their second year when they were a young company with few employees. They often acted on the advice of others in their industry. At times, it was different from their intended direction, but they recognized it was aligned with their vision on how to build value in the marketplace. Resiliency was baked into the culture because they knew the future could be vastly different than the present. Ownership for delivering on commitments and resolving what did not work was reinforced with the motto of "under-promise and over-deliver."

The return on imaginative intelligence and relationships led to continuous improvement in process and resource utilization. The return on cognitive agility propelled HP's growth. The discipline for ongoing situational awareness ensured return on location.

Leadership in the twenty-first century will be rebuilding economies, redefining priorities, and reframing para-digms. We will be faced with unexpected opportuni-ties as we grow out of a worldwide economic setback. *The Integrative Leader Model* provides a solid path for building the needed knowledge and experience. I invite you to empower your organization with a proven approach to leading and providing an expanded opportunity for all who participate in your ecosystem.

APPENDIX A

Acknowledgments

My first acknowledgment goes to my parents, who passed on in 1992 and 2002. They instilled in me a love for learning and communicating. My mother loved a good story, which she found in the many books she read and great movies she enjoyed. Her confidence in my abilities to make a difference with my life has provided me with vision. My father was my first example of personal and professional resilience and profitable entrepreneurship. His journey in life would take him from Durango, Colorado, to Bogota, Colombia, to Boca Raton, Florida. Any challenge brought an opportunity to make lemonade. He was an agile thinker in two languages who operated with a sense of urgency to use time wisely.

To my sister Angela, my lifelong friend and confidante, who was my first thought partner, your success is an example of cognitive diversity. Thank you for your outstanding listening and emotional intelligence skills. You have made it safe for me to share many a contrarian view or imaginative idea yet remain centered and authentic. Your confidence that the information in the book will help many in the future encouraged me to stay on track.

To my brother Edgar, an experienced travel companion, your ability to connect and embrace different cultures and environments reveals how small the world can be if we are willing to understand how others view things.

To my best friend of forty-two years, Barb, the consistency of our connection no matter how different our journey or the length of time in between conversations is a great anchor. Your assistance in editing this book to make it clear and valuable to integrative leaders everywhere is greatly appreciated. Unvarnished feedback teaches by revealing different points of view and builds new neural connections.

To Ann Herrmann, chairwoman and chief thought leader at Herrmann International. Thank you for keeping your father Ned's knowledge about the Whole Brain Model® alive. Understanding your core model helped me tailor mine for coaching business leaders to be effective, resilient, and successful.

To Henry Devries, my publisher, the timing of our connection is an example of kismet. Good partnerships in new endeavors make for good experiences. Your guidance gave me the framework to tell my story. I appreciate you and Indie Books.

To all the leaders I have had the privilege to coach, thank you for including me in your journey. You have made my coaching calling a rewarding profession. The learning between us has been a mutually winning exchange.

To all the professional leaders who took the time to read my drafts and made recommendations for meaningful content, thank you for being outstanding thought partners. I particularly want to thank Susan Wenzel, Carl Nardell, and Steve Neimeister.

APPENDIX B

About The Author

S onia Jeantet is the founder of Cima Executive Development (*cima* is Spanish for peak), a coaching and consulting firm in Southern California; international master personal and executive coach for twenty years, primarily with Fortune 500 companies; and Fortune 100 sales executive with Hewlett-Packard and Digital Equipment Corporation. She has coached more than 300 senior executives to grow and sustain profitable results. Sonia is bilingual in Spanish and English, with strong experience and understanding of cultural differences. She is a Leadership Performance Partner.

Sonia's coaching clients during the past twenty years include Toyota, ADP, Paychex, Raytheon, Johnson & Johnson, Edwards Life Sciences, Equity Residential, Mattel, City National Bank, Warner Bros, Disney, Time Warner, Unified Grocers, Viacom, Gilead Sciences,

TK1SC, Ronald McDonald House Charities of Southern California, Cedars Sinai, and American Association of Critical-Care Nurses.

Her clients' experience includes director through CEO levels in the following disciplines: finance, operations, sales and marketing, human resources, engineering, corporate communications, quality and continuous improvement, and information technology.

Sonia's Coaching Niches

- C-Suite Executive Leadership

- High Potential Development

- Accelerating New Role Transitions

- Executive Successor Readiness

- Women in Leadership

- Executive Presence

- Teams in Action Learning

- Change Management

- Cultural Realignment

Education and Certifications

- MBA, Thunderbird School of Global Management, Arizona State University

- BS, Business, University of Denver

- MPEC (Master Personal & Executive Coach), College of Executive Coaching

APPENDIX C

Works Referenced

Bazigos, Michael, Gagnon, Chris, and Schaninger, Bill. *McKinsey Quarterly:* Leadership in Context. January 2016.

Catmull, Ed. *Creativity Inc.* Random House, 2014.

Drucker, Peter, and *Harvard Business Review* reprint. "What Makes an Effective Executive?" June 2004.

Garvin, David A., Edmondson, Amy C, Gino, Francesca, and Harvard Business Review. "Is Yours a Learning Organization?" March 2008

Hammer, Michael, and *Harvard Business Review.* "The Process Audit." April 2007.

Herrmann Global. Whole Brain Model®. www.thinkherrmann.com

Hill, Dan. *Emotionomics*. Kogan Page, 2007, 2008.

Keller, Scott, Meaney, Mary, and McKinsey & Company. "Successfully transitioning to new leadership roles." May 2018.

Lacy, Peter, LaVelle, Katherine, Zamora, Alberto. "Striking Balance with Whole Brain Leadership – The New Rules of Engagement." Accenture Strategy research study 2019.

Maeda, John. *The Laws of Simplicity*, The MIT Press, 2006.

Malone, Michael S. *Bill & Dave, How Hewlett and Packard Build the World's Greatest Company*, Penguin Group, 2007.

Martin, Jean, Schmidt, Conrad, and *Harvard Business Review*. "How To Keep Your Top Talent." May 2010.

Nace, Trevor. "Earth's Magnetic North Pole Has Officially Moved." *Forbes*. February 5, 2019.

Rock, David. *Quiet Leadership*. HarperCollins, 2006.

Senge, Peter. *Fifth Discipline.* Doubleday, 1994.

Zades, Stephen. *Inc.* "How Creativity Drives Profit, The Sundance Model Can Transform Your Business." September 2003.

INDEX

360 Process, 59

Accenture strategy, 5, 9, 126

American Express, 17-18

Auerbach, Jeff, 25

Beltran, Maria, 23

Bogota, 16, 119

Buffett, Warren, 47

C-suite, 5, 9-11, 80, 124

California, 15, 25, 28, 105, 123-124

Canada, 41

Caribbean, 23

Catmull, Ed, 62, 125

Cedars Sinai, 124

CEO, 5, 36, 41, 51, 61, 124

CFO, 36-37, 50-51

Chief Information Officer, 85

Chief Technology Officer, 85

China, 9

Christmas, 61

City National Bank, 28, 123

Cognitive agility, v, 9, 89-93, 96-98, 100, 105, 109, 117

Cognitive diversity, 4-5, 9-13, 16, 20, 28, 107, 119

Coherence organization, 21, 34, 42, 102, 109

College of Executive Coaching, 124

Colombia, 16, 119

Da Vinci, Leonardo, 103

DEC – Digital Equipment Corporation, 22, 123

Disney, 6, 28, 62, 123

Diversity and inclusion, 80

Drucker, Peter, 51, 125

Emotional intelligence, 7, 77-78, 80, 120

Enterprise maturity model, 67, 73

Executive Coach, 6, 13, 24, 26, 28, 52, 123-124

FAA - Federal Aviation Administration, 32

Forbes, 31, 126

Fortune 100, 68, 123

Fortune 400, 47

Fortune 500, 6, 28, 50, 123

France, 9

Germany, 9, 47

Goleman, Daniel, 78

GPS, 32

Grove, Andy, 55

Hammer, Michael, 67, 73, 125

Harvard Business Review, 51, 73, 98, 101, 107, 125-126

Herrmann Global, 5, 125

Hewlett, Bill, 115

Hewlett-Packard, 18, 20, 123

High-potential executives, 6, 7, 52

Hill, Dan - Emotionomics, 79, 126

HP Way, 19-20, 116

HR - Human Resources, 13, 27-28, 65, 80, 124

Inc. magazine, 61

Integrative Leadership Model, iii, 9, 12-13

Intel, 55

IPO, 39, 62

Italy, 9

Laguna, 23

Latin America, 17

Maeda, John - Laws of Simplicity, 96, 126

Malone, Michael, 19, 126

MBA - Master of Business Administration, 17, 46, 124

McKinsey Quarterly, 34, 41, 125

Nace, Trevor, 31, 126

NASA, 32

New rules of engagement for the C-suite, 10

North Pole, 31-32, 126

Packard, Dave, 115

Palo Alto, 21

Pixar, 62

QuickBooks, 26

Quiet Leadership, 8, 126

Ratey, John, 17

Raytheon, 6, 28, 123

Redford, Robert, 61

Rock, David, 8, 126

Rockwell International, 21

ROI - Return on Investment, v, 6, 45-46, 51, 104, 33, 46-48, 52

Russia, 31

Senge, Peter - Fifth Discipline, 42, 126

Spanish, 16, 28, 123

STEM - Science, Technology Engineering and Mathematics, 68

Sundance, 61-62, 126

SWOT analysis, 43

The Whole Brain Thinking Model, 5

Thunderbird School of Global Management, Arizona State University, 124

Toyota, 28, 123

UCI - University of California Irvine, 15

UK, 9-10

University of Denver, 53, 124

US Forest Service, 32

Venezuelan, 23

Warner Bros., 6, 28

Whole-brain, vii, 4, 7, 9-11, 17, 106

Zades, Stephen, 61, 126

www.ingramcontent.com/pod-product-compliance
Lightning Source LLC
Chambersburg PA
CBHW040901210326
41597CB00029B/4926